# ENDORSEMENTS

In a day when being "spiritual" is in vogue, there are many ideas about what meditation is all about. Many of those ideas involve all sorts of techniques to put the practitioner into a posture of receptivity. Scripturally, meditation has a focus and an object. It isn't a mantra that is repeated over and over again in an effort to achieve a higher level of consciousness. Rather it is a process of ruminating on the Word of God in the mind. In the same way a cow "chews the cud," so Biblical meditation requires coming to the Scriptures and "chewing over them" again and again in prayerful, reflective contemplation, learning to ask questions of the Holy Spirit while doing so, and quietly and receptively receiving illumination from Him regarding all the rich treasures hidden in Christ that He wants to reveal to us. Mark Virkler has spent his journey inviting us to see, hear, experience, and know God in Christ. In this latest treasure-trove from his life, *Hearing God Through Biblical Meditation* he puts communion with God within your reach and grasp. He spreads a banquet table for you in the midst of the conflicts and decisions of life that you are facing. Happy feasting!

BISHOP MARK J. CHIRONNA, MA. PhD
Mark Chironna Ministries
Church On The Living Edge
Orlando, Florida

*Hearing God Through Biblical Meditation* is a straightforward book that instructs the reader with clear words and easy-to-follow exercises. The value of the book is found in the *doing* rather than in the *reading* of it. A good reader can completely read it in a few hours, but remain unchanged. A wise student will put it into practice, without regard for how long the exercises may take. It is not simply a book to be consumed and placed on the shelf; it is a call to make a place for its practice to be authentically incorporated into everyday life. This is how God's voice can be heard.

REV. JOHN R. MILLER, Ph.D.
Elim Bible Institute & College, Lima, NY
Regent University, Virginia Beach, VA

My life and spiritual journey were transformed as a result of hearing God's voice. The man who taught me this skill set was Mark Virkler. As a rational person I was guided by Mark to understand amazing keys that our Scriptures reveal to us. Mark also is masterful at providing practical tools that allow us to hear the Shepherd's voice. Mark's newest book, *Hearing God Through Biblical Meditation*, takes us another step deeper in this wonderful journey of hearing God. Being still and knowing God experientially is a profound and life changing truth. Mark helps us unpack the theology of meditation and then takes us on a journey to discover more of God's heart.

STEVE LONG
Senior Leader, Catch the Fire Toronto

Dr. Mark Virkler's new book, *Hearing God through Biblical Meditation* may be the most important read of this generation. Now more than ever believers need to continually interact with God through communication. God is speaking but the church has dulled the ears of its members. This book is an awakening of the spiritual ear. Dr. Mark is a pioneer—at times a lonely voice—yet one who has taught countless individuals over many years to hear God's voice. Get ready for what might be the last great awakening as you read this book and activate your inner ear.

DR. JOHN LOUIS MURATORI
Bestselling author *Money by Design*

I am glad to recommend Dr. Mark Virkler's book, *Hearing God Through Biblical Meditation*. Dr. Virkler is a trusted teacher in this area of revelation, and people around the world have been blessed and touched by putting into practice the simp=le concepts he presents here. You will hear God's voice by receiving the truths in this book.

Dr. Randy Clark, D Min.,
President and Founder of Global Awakening

*Hearing God Through Biblical Meditation* brings together in a clear, easy to understand format, how to experience the power of hearing God's voice. Dr. Virkler is one of our regular faculty members at Global School of Supernatural Ministry, and the concepts he presents in this book have assisted our students in hearing the voice of God. I highly recommend this book to anyone who desires to more clearly hear from God, and develop a deeper, more intimate fellowship with Him!"

Dr. Michael Hutchings, D Min,
Director of Global School of Supernatural Ministry and
Global Certification Education Programs

GOD

*through*

BIBLICAL MEDITATION

*unlocking*

FRESH REVELATION

DAILY

MARK VIRKLER

DESTINY IMAGE® PUBLISHERS, INC.

P.O. Box 310, Shippensburg, PA 17257-0310

*"Promoting Inspired Lives."*

This book and all other Destiny Image and Destiny Image Fiction books are available at Christian bookstores and distributors worldwide.

Cover design by Eileen Rockwell

For more information on foreign distributors, call 717-532-3040.

Reach us on the Internet: www.destinyimage.com.

ISBN 13 TP: 978-0-7684-0881-2
ISBN 13 eBook: 978-0-7684-0882-9

For Worldwide Distribution, Printed in the U.S.A.

1 2 3 4 5 6 7 8 / 20 19 18 17 16

# CONTENTS

# FOREWORD

Mark Virkler's new project, *Hearing God through Biblical Meditation*, forces the reader to confront the most basic temptation of humanity: *Do we heed the words of men or the voice of God?* (See Genesis 3; Exodus 20; Matthew 4; Luke 4.)

Our current "ministry training" system (seminaries and even Bible schools) focus on learning the "facts" of Scripture and lists of doctrines—*creeds*. Indeed, Jesus attacks the seminary professors of His day by showing that they were obsessed with substituting a knowledge of Bible facts for the content of the Great Covenant that God was offering in that Bible—the very voice of God, the "law of God written in the heart," revealed.

Jesus said in John 5:37–40,

> *The Father who sent me has himself borne witness about me* [in mighty works]. *His voice you have never heard, his form you have never seen, and you do not have his word abiding in you, for you do not believe the one whom he has sent. You search the Scriptures because you think that in them you have eternal life; and it is they that bear witness about me, yet you refuse to come to me that you may have life* (ESV).

This is exactly the message Mark Virkler is laying out in *Hearing God through Biblical Meditation*. If we read the Bible correctly, it will reveal Jesus and our relationship with Him—a relationship that necessarily involves communication, hearing His voice.

Jesus's mission is introduced in all four Gospels as the One who will "baptize in the Holy Spirit," that is, who will turn us into prophets who can hear and speak God's words. This was the essence of the New Covenant in Jeremiah 31:31–34, Second Corinthians 3, and Isaiah 59:21, cited as the climax of the most important sermon in Christianity—the Pentecost sermon in Acts 2:39.

In this interactive work, Mark Virkler nails the most important function of the Scriptures—to *reveal Jesus.*

JON RUTHVEN
Author, *What's Wrong with Protestant Theology:
Traditions vs. Biblical Emphasis* and
*On the Cessation of the Charismata*

# How to Hear God's Voice

She had done it again! Instead of coming straight home from school like she was supposed to, she had gone to her friend's house. Without permission. Without our knowledge. Without doing her chores.

With a ministering household that included remnants of three struggling families plus our own toddler and newborn, my wife simply couldn't handle all the work on her own. Everyone had to pull their own weight. Everyone had age-appropriate tasks they were expected to complete. At fourteen, Rachel and her younger brother were living with us while her parents tried to overcome lifestyle patterns that had resulted in the children running away to escape the dysfunction. I felt sorry for Rachel, but honestly, my wife was my greatest concern.

Now Rachel had ditched her chores to spend time with her friends. It wasn't the first time, but if I had anything to say about it, it would be the last. I intended to lay down the law when she got home and make it very clear that if she was going to live under my roof, she would obey my rules.

But…she wasn't home yet. And I had recently been learning to hear God's voice more clearly. Maybe I should try to see if I could hear anything from Him about the situation. Maybe He could give me a way to get her to do what she was supposed to (i.e., what I wanted her to do). So I went to my office and reviewed what the Lord had been teaching me from Habakkuk 2:1-2: "I will stand on my guard post and station myself on the rampart; and I will keep watch to see what He will speak to me…. Then the Lord answered me and said, 'Record the vision.'"

Habakkuk said, "I will stand on my guard post." *The first key to hearing God's voice is to go to a quiet place and still our own thoughts and emotions.* Psalm 46:10 encourages us to be still, let go, cease striving, and know that He is God. In Psalm 37:7 we are called to "Rest in the Lord and wait patiently for Him." There is a deep inner knowing in our spirits that each of us can experience when we quiet our flesh and our minds. Practicing the art of biblical meditation helps silence the outer noise and distractions clamoring for our attention.

I didn't have a guard post but I did have an office, so I went there to quiet my temper and my mind. Loving God through a quiet worship song is one very effective way to become still. In Second Kings, Elisha needed a word from the Lord, so he said, "Bring me a minstrel," and as the minstrel played, the Lord spoke (2 Kings 3:15). I have found that playing a worship song on my autoharp is the quickest way for me to come to stillness. I need to choose my song carefully; boisterous songs of praise do not bring me to stillness, but rather gentle songs that express my love and worship. And it isn't enough just to sing the song into the cosmos. I come into the Lord's presence most quickly and easily when I use my godly imagination to see the truth that He is right here with me and I sing my songs to Him, personally.

"I will keep watch to see," said the prophet. To receive the pure word of God, it is very important that my heart be properly focused as I become still, because my focus is the source of the intuitive flow.

If I fix my eyes upon Jesus (Heb. 12:2), the intuitive flow comes from Jesus. But if I fix my gaze upon some desire of my heart, the intuitive flow comes out of that desire. To have a pure flow I must become still and carefully fix my eyes upon Jesus. Quietly worshiping the King and receiving out of the stillness that follows quite easily accomplishes this.

So I used *the second key to hearing God's voice: As you pray, fix the eyes of your heart upon Jesus, seeing in the Spirit the dreams and visions of Almighty God.* Habakkuk was actually looking for vision as he prayed. He opened the eyes of his heart and looked into the spirit world to see what God wanted to show him.

God has always spoken through dreams and visions, and He specifically said that they would come to those upon whom the Holy Spirit is poured out (Acts 2:1–4, 17).

Being a logical, rational person, observable facts that could be verified by my physical senses were the foundations of my life, including my spiritual life. I had never thought of opening the eyes of my heart and looking for vision. However, I have come to believe that this is exactly what God wants me to do. He gave me eyes in my heart to see in the spirit the vision and movement of Almighty God. There is an active spirit world all around us full of angels, demons, the Holy Spirit, the omnipresent Father, and His omnipresent Son, Jesus. The only reasons for me not to see this reality are unbelief or lack of knowledge.

In his sermon in Acts 2:25, Peter refers to King David's statement: "I saw the Lord always in my presence; for He is at my right hand, so that I will not be shaken." The original psalm makes it clear that this was a decision of David's, not a constant supernatural visitation: "I have set (literally, *I have placed*) the Lord continually before me; because He is at my right hand, I will not be shaken" (Ps. 16:8). Because David knew that the Lord was always with him, he determined in his spirit to *see* that truth with the eyes of his heart as he went through life, knowing that this would keep his faith strong.

In order to see, we must look. Daniel saw a vision in his mind and said, "I was looking" and "I kept looking" (Dan. 7:2,9,13). As I pray, I look for Jesus, and I watch as He speaks to me, doing and saying the things that are on His heart. Many Christians will find that if they will only look, they will see. Jesus is Emmanuel, God with us (Matt. 1:23). It is as simple as that. You can see Christ present with you because Christ *is* present with you. In fact, the vision may come so easily that you will be tempted to reject it, thinking that it is just you. But if you persist in recording these visions, your doubt will soon be overcome by faith as you recognize that the content of them could only be birthed in Almighty God.

Jesus demonstrated the ability of living out of constant contact with God, declaring that He did nothing on His own initiative, but only what He saw the Father doing, and heard the Father saying (John 5:19-20,30). What an incredible way to live!

Is it possible for us to live out of divine initiative as Jesus did? Yes! We must simply fix our eyes upon Jesus. The veil has been torn, giving access into the immediate presence of God, and He calls us to draw near (Luke 23:45; Heb. 10:19-22). "I pray that the eyes of your heart may be enlightened" (Eph. 1:18).

When I had quieted my heart enough that I was able to picture Jesus without the distractions of my own ideas and plans, I was able to "keep watch to see what He will speak to me." I wrote down my question: "Lord, what should I do about Rachel?"

Immediately the thought came to me, "She is insecure." Well, that certainly wasn't my thought! Her behavior looked like rebellion to me, not insecurity.

But like Habakkuk, I was coming to know the sound of God speaking to me (Hab. 2:2). Elijah described it as a still, small voice (1 Kings 19:12 NKJV). I had previously listened for an inner audible voice, and God does speak that way at times. However, I have found that usually, God's voice comes as spontaneous thoughts, visions, feelings, or impressions.

For example, haven't you been driving down the road and had a thought come to you to pray for a certain person? Didn't you believe it was God telling you to pray? What did God's voice sound like? Was it an audible voice, or was it a spontaneous thought that lit upon your mind?

Experience indicates that we perceive spirit-level communication as spontaneous thoughts, impressions, and visions, and Scripture confirms this in many ways. For example, one definition of *paga*, a Hebrew word for intercession, is "a chance encounter or an accidental intersecting." When God lays people on our hearts, He does it through *paga*, a chance-encounter thought "accidentally" intersecting our minds.

So *the third key to hearing God's voice is recognizing that God's voice in your heart often sounds like a flow of spontaneous thoughts.* Therefore, when I want to hear from God, I tune to chance-encounter or spontaneous thoughts.

Finally, God told Habakkuk to record the vision (Hab. 2:2). This was not an isolated command. The Scriptures record many examples of individual's prayers and God's replies, such as the Psalms, many of the prophets, and Revelation. I have found that obeying this final principle amplified my confidence in my ability to hear God's voice so that I could finally make living out of His initiatives a way of life. The *fourth key, two-way journaling or the writing out of your prayers and God's answers, brings great freedom in hearing God's voice.*

I have found two-way journaling to be a fabulous catalyst for clearly discerning God's inner, spontaneous flow, because as I journal I am able to write in faith for long periods of time, simply believing it is God. I know that what I believe I have received from God must be tested. However, testing involves doubt and doubt blocks divine communication, so I do not want to test while I am trying to receive (James 1:5–8). With journaling, I can receive in faith, knowing that when the flow has ended I can test and examine it carefully.

So I wrote down what I believed He had said: "She is insecure."

But the Lord wasn't done. I continued to write the spontaneous thoughts that came to me: "Love her unconditionally. She is flesh of your flesh and bone of your bone."

My mind immediately objected: *She is not flesh of my flesh. She is not related to me at all—she is a foster child, just living in my home temporarily.* It was definitely time to test this "word from the Lord"!

There are three possible sources of thoughts in our minds—ourselves, satan, and the Holy Spirit. It was obvious that the words in my journal did not come from my own mind; I certainly didn't see her as insecure *or* flesh of my flesh. And I sincerely doubted that satan would encourage me to love anyone unconditionally!

Okay, it was starting to look like I might have actually received counsel from the Lord. It was consistent with the names and character of God as revealed in the Scripture, and totally contrary to the names and character of the enemy. So that meant that I was hearing from the Lord, and He wanted me to see the situation in a different light. Rachel was my daughter—part of my family, not by blood but by the hand of God Himself. The chaos of her birth home had created deep insecurity about her worthiness to be loved by anyone, including me and including God. Only the unconditional love of the Lord expressed through an imperfect human would reach her heart.

But there was still one more test I needed to perform before I would have absolute confidence that this was truly God's word to me: I needed confirmation from someone else whose spiritual discernment I trusted. So I went to my wife and shared what I had received. I knew if I could get her validation, especially as she was the one most wronged in the situation, then I could say, at least to myself, "Thus sayeth the Lord."

Needless to say, Patti immediately and without question confirmed that the Lord had spoken to me. My entire planned lecture was forgotten. I returned to my office anxious to hear more. As the Lord planted a new, supernatural love for Rachel within me, He showed me what to say and how to say it to not only address the current issue of household responsibility, but the deeper issues of love and acceptance and worthiness.

Rachel and her brother remained as part of our family for another two years, giving us many opportunities to demonstrate and teach about the Father's love, planting spiritual seeds in thirsty soil. We weren't perfect and we didn't solve all of her issues, but because I had learned to listen to the Lord, we were able to avoid creating more brokenness and separation.

The four simple keys that the Lord showed me from Habakkuk have been used by people of all ages—from four to a hundred and four, from every continent, culture, and denomination—to break through into intimate, two-way conversations with their loving Father and dearest Friend. Omitting any one of the keys will prevent you from receiving all He wants to say to you. The order of the keys is not important, just that you *use them all*. Embracing all four by faith can change your life. Simply quiet yourself down, tune to spontaneity, look for vision, and journal. He is waiting to meet you there.

You will be amazed when you journal! Doubt may hinder you at first, but throw it off, reminding yourself that it is a biblical concept and that God is present, speaking to His children. Relax. When we cease our labors and enter His rest, God is free to flow (Heb. 4:10).

Why not try it for yourself, right now? Sit back comfortably, take out your pen and paper, and smile. Turn your attention toward the Lord in praise and worship, seeking His face. Many people have found the music and visionary prayer called "A Stroll Along the Sea of Galilee" helpful in getting them started. You can listen to it and download it free at www.cwgministries.org/galilee.

After you write your question to the Lord, become still, fixing your gaze on Jesus. You will suddenly have a very good thought. Don't doubt it; simply write it down. Later, as you read your journaling, you, too, will be blessed to discover that you are indeed dialoguing with God. If you wonder if it is really the Lord speaking to you, share it with your spouse, friend, or spiritual mentor. Their input will encourage your faith and strengthen your commitment to spend time getting to know the Lover of your soul more intimately than you ever dreamed possible.

# IS IT REALLY GOD SPEAKING?

As you embark upon this journey of experiencing God's presence through the pages of Scripture, I want to give you five ways to be sure that what you are hearing through your biblical meditation is actually coming from God.

## 1. Test the Origin (1 John 4:1)

Thoughts from our own minds are progressive, with one thought leading to the next, however tangentially. Thoughts from the spirit world are spontaneous. The Hebrew word for true prophecy is *naba*, which literally means to bubble up, whereas false prophecy is *ziyd* meaning to boil up. True words from the Lord will bubble up from our innermost being; we don't need to cook them up ourselves.

## 2. Compare It to Biblical Principles

God will never say something to you personally which is contrary to His universal revelation as expressed in the Scriptures. If the Bible clearly states that something is a sin, no amount of journaling can make it right. Much of what you journal about will not be specifically addressed in the Bible, however, so an understanding of biblical principles is also needed.

### 3. *Compare It to the Names and Character of God as Revealed in the Bible*

Anything God says to you will be in harmony with His essential nature. Journaling will help you get to *know* God personally, but knowing what the Bible says *about* Him will help you discern what words are from Him. They will represent His very nature. Even though the details of what you are journaling may not be specifically expressed in Scripture, the essence of what God is revealing to you will always be in agreement with His attributes. Make sure the tenor of your journaling lines up with the character of God as described in the names of the Father, Son, and Holy Spirit.

### 4. *Test the Fruit (Matthew 7:15–20)*

What effect does what you are hearing have on your soul and your spirit? Words from the Lord will quicken your faith and increase your love, peace, and joy. They will stimulate a sense of humility within you as you become more aware of who God is and who you are. On the other hand, any words you receive that cause you to fear or doubt, bring you into confusion or anxiety, or stroke your ego (especially if you hear something that is "just for you alone—no one else is worthy") must be immediately rebuked and rejected as lies of the enemy.

### 5. *Share It with Your Spiritual Counselors (Proverbs 11:14)*

We are members of a Body! A cord of three strands is not easily broken, and God's intention has always been for us to grow together. Nothing will increase your faith in your ability to hear from God like having it confirmed by two or three other people! Share it with your spouse, your parents, your friends, your elder, your group leader, even your grown children can be your sounding board. They don't need to be perfect or super-spiritual; they just need to love you, be committed to being available to you, have a solid biblical orientation, and most importantly, they must also willingly and easily receive counsel. Avoid the authoritarian who insists that because of their standing in the church or with God, they no longer need to listen to others. Find two or three people and let them confirm that you are hearing from God!

The four keys to hearing God's voice, along with this five-step evaluation process, will serve as the foundation for what you will be exploring in the pages ahead concerning biblical meditation.

# How Does One Discover Truth from Scripture?

I wrote this book because for many years I studied the Bible incorrectly, and it produced death rather than life. Even though I had a knowledge of the Scriptures, I did not personally experience the life and the realities they revealed. The Bible calls this the ministry of death, rather than the ministry of righteousness (2 Cor. 3:6–9). Upon coming out of Bible college, I found myself just like the apostle Paul, attacking those who disagreed with my theology.

I want to help you *avoid* these pitfalls; I want to help you learn how to experience the Word of God to where you are no longer merely reading words on a page, but it is like the voice of the Holy Spirit is speaking to you—clearly and consistently—through the Scriptures. Is this possible? Absolutely.

Once I learned to hear God's voice, I let God lead me to the Scriptures, I let God reveal the Scriptures to my heart, and I experienced what the disciples experienced—my heart burning within as Jesus opened up Scriptures for me (Luke 24:32). This is what I believe you will experience as you learn how to practice biblical meditation and start attaching expectation to reading the Scriptures. In other words, when you read the Bible, you begin to expect encounters with the Holy Spirit. You expect to hear God speaking to you. It's no longer a draining chore, but a delightful adventure!

When this happened for me, Bible verses started leaping off the page, revelation was flashing, and I discovered this could happen every single day, every time I opened the Bible—or any book for that matter. God knows a lot about a lot of topics, and He is able to grant revelation in every area I read if I approach the book with the proper heart attitude. What an insight!

Now you can receive revelation knowledge in each and every area, all the time, simply by inviting the Holy Spirit to be a vital part of the learning process. You will become like David, who wrote, "Oh how I love your law! It is my meditation *all the day*" (Ps. 119:97 ESV).

*So now, I want to teach you this process.* I want Bible verses to start leaping off the page every time *you* read the Bible or any other book. Perhaps you have heard pastors or ministry leaders speak of experiences like this, where the Bible came alive to them and God gave them inspiration for a sermon, a message, or some kind of prophetic word. I want you to know, right up front, that this kind of experience is *not* reserved for those in ministry. I am not someone who has attained or achieved some kind of unique experience; God wants to communicate with *all* of His beloved children. This includes you!

I encourage you to read on and discover how to posture your heart and mind properly so this wonderful miracle of divine encounter happens for you every single day for the rest of your life. The days of straining to hear God are coming to an end, and you will discover how easy it is to hear from Heaven simply by opening the Scriptures and meditating on their truths.

*Biblical meditation is not off-limits.* As soon as people start using the word *meditation*, I know it makes some Christians a bit nervous. This is because of how Eastern religion and the New Age movement have presented their counterfeit version. It is very important that just because we see a counterfeit of a biblical truth, we do *not* throw out the biblical truth altogether. As I say, no one makes counterfeit one-dollar bills; they copy the larger denominations. In the same way, the devil works very intentionally to counterfeit scriptural truths that have the strongest potential to bring the people of God into greater levels of intimacy with God and clarity in hearing the Holy Spirit. Meditation is one of these key truths.

> *This Book of the Law shall not depart from your mouth, but you shall **meditate** in it day and night, that you may observe to do according to all that is written in it. For then you will make your way prosperous, and then you will have good success* (Joshua 1:8 NKJV).

> *I will also **meditate** on all Your work, And talk of Your deeds* (Psalm 77:12 NKJV).

> *Do not neglect the gift that is in you, which was given to you by prophecy with the laying on of the hands of the eldership. **Meditate** on these things; give yourself entirely to them, that your progress may be evident to all. Take heed to yourself and to the doctrine. Continue in them, for in doing this you will save both yourself and those who hear you* (1 Timothy 4:14–16 NKJV).

Throughout this book, I will be giving you many scriptural examples that validate and encourage biblical meditation.

## YOUR GOAL

This book, like *Hearing God*, is presented as both an informative and interactive study. I am purposefully *not* offering a book that is *all* teaching because I want you to practice the process. By the end of this journey, I want you to feel comfortable with the biblical meditation process, and most of all, I want you to have a new sense of expectancy when you approach the Bible, that God will speak through its pages.

Each segment in the book is easy to read, providing both information and opportunity for interaction. Your goal is to activate the process of biblical meditation. At the end of many of the segments, you will have some reflection questions and a Scripture passage to meditate on. You will not have reflection questions and meditation exercises for every segment, as there are some that will prove to be strictly informational—particularly the last section, which focuses on mistakes to avoid when approaching biblical meditation.

In addition, I will provide a sample of what the seven-step process looks like. My hope is that you will take the information you learn in each segment and apply it to your meditation Scripture. Watch the Bible come to life like never before as you *surrender* trying to figure it out through natural human study and instead let the Holy Spirit guide the process.

You will also read testimonies and stories of people who meditated on Scripture and how God spoke to them through what they were reading. It is my hope that these stories build your faith and give you practical examples of what the process looks like. The last thing we want to do is make biblical meditation seem obscure, hyper-spiritual, and exclusive to only a select, superior few. On the contrary, it should be a vital part of our everyday Christian lives!

And do your friends a favor. Share these wonderful, simple truths with them also. It is unfortunate to watch so many Christians approach their time in the Bible with religious formalism, zero expectation, and a rigid sense of obligation. God wants to transform this. In the pages ahead, I believe He will start with you. Then, as you put these simple keys into practice in your life, people will want to hear God and enjoy His Word the same way that you do!

In the journey ahead, we will answer the following questions:

1.  Is there a difference between biblical meditation and western study?

2.  Where do inductive Bible study methods fit into biblical meditation?

3.  If I approach the Bible *the way God intended*, will it produce spirit and life (John 6:63)?

4.  If I approach the Bible without the Spirit, will it produce the "ministry of condemnation" and death (2 Cor. 3:7–9)?

5.  What principle allows the New Testament writers to apply Old Testament verses out of context? Am I allowed to use this same principle with both Old and New Testament verses?

6.  Are the verses *really* true: "It is the Spirit who gives life; the flesh profits *nothing*" (John 6:63), and man's thoughts are not God's thoughts (Isa. 55:8-9)? Does that mean that Bible study which is done in my strength and with the straining of my mind is what Paul called "dung" (Phil. 3:8 KJV)?

7.  Does the Bible really say that meditation on God's laws results in making my way prosperous and successful?

As you move forward, I encourage you to pick up a pen, find some blank paper to journal on (we will be providing some in this book), and pray these simple words to Father God:

*Father, Your words are spirit and they are life! I approach the Bible in a new way today. I don't come out of obligation; I come with expectation! I don't open this book because I am forced to, or because I think reading Your Word gives me more favor with You. It does not. Your Word helps me to know You deeply and experience You fully!*

*Today, I invite You, Spirit of God, to come and lead me in this journey of biblical meditation. Open my eyes to see Your truth in a fresh way. Open my ears to hear Your voice as You desire to speak to me through these pages.*

*Thank You, Lord, for what You are going to do in my life through this journey. I know my relationship with You will never be the same because I am going to learn how to hear Your voice in a way that I never have before. You are increasing the clarity. You are increasing the volume. You are increasing the consistency.*

*And finally, thank You Jesus—You died on the cross to forgive me of sin and make it possible for me to hear the Father's voice all of the time. You died so that I could be filled with the very Spirit of God, who You promised would be my helper, friend, and comforter forever. Holy Spirit, You are my constant companion in this journey. Thank You for showing me how to meditate on Scripture and hear from Heaven like never before.*

*In Jesus's name,*

*Amen.*

**Let the journey into biblical meditation begin!**

THE ESSENCE OF MY BELIEF IS THAT THERE IS A difference, a vast difference between fact and truth. Truth in the Scriptures is more than a fact. A fact may be detached, impersonal, cold and totally disassociated from life. Truth, on the other hand is warm, living and spiritual. *A theological fact may be held in the mind for a lifetime without its having any positive effect upon the moral character; but truth is creative, saving, transforming and it always changes the one who received it into a humbler and holier man.*

Theological facts are like the altar of Elijah on Mount Carmel before the fire came; correct, properly laid out but altogether cold. When the heart makes the ultimate surrender, the fire falls and true facts are transmuted into spiritual truth that transforms, enlightens and sanctifies. *The church or the individual that is Bible taught without being Spirit taught has simply failed to see that truth lies deeper than the theological statement of it. We only possess what we experience!*

—A.W. TOZER

# *Part One*

# AN INTRODUCTION TO BIBLICAL MEDITATION

*This book of the law shall not depart from your mouth, but you shall meditate on it day and night, so that you may be careful to do according to all that is written in it; for then you will make your way prosperous, and then you will have success.*

—JOSHUA 1:8

*Give yourself to prayer, to reading and meditation on divine truths: strive to penetrate to the bottom of them and never be content with a superficial knowledge.*

—DAVID BRAINERD

# An Encounter in Psalm 139

## UMC Church Pastor Arthur Wesley asks:
### *What do You want to say to me, Lord?*

*We have had a good day and there are more blessings to come. My love is new every day, always present, active, and surrounds you with mercy and loving kindness. I am aware of your heart and thoughts (Psalm 139). It pleases Me when you often think of Me and My word, My people, and ponder My ways. This is how you grow in intimacy and boldness.*

*Things are blossoming in your life that have lain dormant. A **new season** is here, a season of wonderful growth and discovery. Drink in My Spirit, drink in deeply. Smell the fragrance of My love and presence. I will heighten your spiritual senses. Soon you will see angels who abide with you always.*

*I have many children but few sons and daughters who will truly listen to Me or pay attention to their hearts. Pay attention to your heart; look deep within and hear Me. This is not weird or unusual but normal for all who seek to know Me, not just with their mind or will but with their heart and spirit. I am Spirit; those who know Me must know Me through spirit. That is where I dwell.*

*You cannot know Me through intellectual reasoning or abstract, detached thinking. I am not data to be studied or a thing to be observed. I am alive, full of emotion, passion, love, goodness, and truth. I am not like a science to be learned and studied and mastered. Relationships are not the same. They do not follow logical patterns but contain mystery. Know the mystery of who I AM. I will teach you these things as I have over the past 40 years, but now it will be much clearer to you. Soon you will experience new realms of My presence and glory.*

*Thank you for listening today.*

*Chapter 1*

# ACCESS SPIRITUAL REALITIES

Before you begin to engage the meditation process, I want you to become mindful of a few key terms that I will be referring to throughout the book.

1. **God's Voice**—Spontaneous thoughts that light upon our minds while our hearts are fixed on Jesus

2. **Living Truth**—Truth that is revealed by the Holy Spirit and has become radiant in one's life

3. **A Living Relationship with the Subject**—A love, passion, and internalized mastery of the principles

4. **A Spirit-Anointed Teacher**—Has a living relationship with the subject at hand and invites his students into that relationship, as full partners, to experience their own living relationship with the subject

5. **Spirit-Anointed Teaching**—Creating space where revelation knowledge and the Holy Spirit's power are experienced and practiced

6. **Western Study**—Man's use of his rational abilities

7. **Biblical Meditation**—The Holy Spirit's use of every faculty of man's heart and mind

# REFLECT

In the space below, I want you to write down the *difference* between simply reading the Bible and having a *living relationship with the subject.*

What does this look like to you?

_____

_____

_____

_____

_____

_____

_____

_____

_____

_____

_____

_____

_____

_____

_____

_____

_____

_____

_____

_____

_____

_____

_____

What do you think *spirit-anointed teaching* sounds/feels like? Pause and take a moment to remember a time in your life when you received information (preached, taught, reading a book) and it seemed to be *more* than information—you actually felt something on the teaching. Perhaps you have experienced this multiple times. Take one key instance where this happened and vividly recall it, for that is an example of biblical information taking on a spiritual dimension. You heard God's voice communicating as it came through the vehicle of a teaching, sermon, book, or presentation. In the same way, the Holy Spirit wants *you* to personally hear His voice through reading the Scriptures.

_____

_____

_____

_____

_____

_____

_____

_____

_____

_____

_____

_____

_____

_____

_____

_____

_____

_____

_____

_____

_____

# DAILY SCRIPTURE MEDITATION

*Isaac went out to meditate in the field toward evening; and he lifted up his eyes and looked, and behold, camels were coming* (Genesis 24:63).

Consider the whole story in its context. This entire chapter of Genesis 24 is about Isaac finding a bride—who is ultimately Rebekah.

# MEDITATION PROMPTS

- Where do you think verse 63 fits into the unfolding of this story?

- How do you think the process of meditation fit into Isaac's life?

- Do you think there is any connection between biblical meditation and the process of spiritually *lifting your eyes* to see what God is doing in your life? In the world?

*Chapter 2*

# YOUR QUEST FOR ENCOUNTER

Are you *hungry* to hear God's voice? If so, you are in the right place! This is the posture of meditation; it must be a wholehearted pursuit of the Person of Truth, God Himself.

Today, I want you to start building an expectation for hearing and finding God in the Scriptures. Review the following process that begins with searching and ends with your prosperity and success.

Remember, God does not stir up a desire within you only to leave you unsatisfied and unfulfilled. He stirs hunger in your heart so you seek Him, find Him, receive revelation, and walk in fruitfulness in every area of your life.

- **Wholehearted searching**: "You will seek Me and find Me when you search for Me with all your heart" (Jer. 29:13).

- **Diligent searchers find Him**: "Those who diligently seek me will find me" (Prov. 8:17).

- **His revelation is a gift of grace**: "If you seek Him, He will let you find Him" (1 Chron. 28:9).

- **Experiencing a burning within**: Our hearts burn within as Jesus opens Scriptures to us (Luke 24:32).

- **Revelation results in fruitfulness**: "In His law he meditates day and night. He will be like a tree firmly planted by streams of water, which yields its fruit in its season and its leaf does not wither; and in whatever he does, he prospers" (Ps. 1:2-3).

- **Revelation results in prosperity and success**: "This book of the law shall not depart from your mouth, but you shall meditate on it day and night, so that you may be careful to do according to all that is written in it; for then you will make your way prosperous, and then you will have success" (Josh. 1:8).

# REFLECT

Consider the process I just listed. *Where do you find yourself along the journey?* Perhaps you are in the whole-hearted searching category. Remember, God Himself wants to be the end goal of your search! He wants to satisfy and fulfill the desire for Himself that He awakened within you. He is a good Father and He rewards those who diligently seek Him!

> Coming to truth is not man's accomplishment; it is God pouring out revelation. Meditation ushers in revelation, which ushers in prosperity and success. Coming to truth is coming to Him and receiving from Him—an obtainment, not an attainment.

Perhaps you are not there. Maybe you don't even *feel* hungry for God or don't find yourself pursuing Him right now...but you want to. In fact, the cry of your heart is, "Lord, I *want* to pursue You." Celebrate this! God is actually moving and working in your heart, for only He can awaken this cry. If you are hungry for God, pursue Him. If you are not hungry for God—but want to be—pursue Him! Either way, He is awakening desire in you. He wants you to clearly hear His voice so you can walk in revelation and enjoy complete fruitfulness.

Maybe you *are hungry* for God and you *are pursuing Him*, but you want to hear His voice with greater clarity and want to enjoy your time in the Bible more.

Take this time to evaluate *where you are* on the journey and write it out in the space below.

_____

_____

_____

_____

_____

_____

_____

_____

_____

_____

_____

This is your starting point. Celebrate it! From this point onward, God only wants to take you deeper and open your spiritual ears to hear Him with *greater* clarity. I encourage you, start to attach expectation to your time in the Word!

## DAILY SCRIPTURE MEDITATION

*You will seek Me and find Me when you search for Me with all your heart* (Jeremiah 29:13).

## MEDITATION PROMPTS

- What does it look like to seek God with *all* of your heart?

- Describe the level of expectation that you should have when searching for God.

- How can you search for God when you already have God (Holy Spirit) living inside of you?

# YOUR GLORY IS TO SEARCH AND FIND THE KING

You might be asking, How do I meditate on Scripture and receive life-transforming revelation?

You're hungry for God.

You're pursuing Him, asking the Holy Spirit to stir up new levels of expectation in your heart.

You're now getting ready to approach the Word of God...and meditate on it.

What does this look like?

"Is meditation simply me studying harder?"

"Is meditation a New Age or Eastern technique?"

The answer to both questions is *no!*

 **BIBLICAL MEDITATION**

*"God's Spirit utilizing every faculty of my heart and mind, bringing forth revelation which ushers in transformation."*

*It is the glory of God to conceal a matter, but the glory of kings is to search out a matter* (Proverbs 25:2).

Through biblical meditation, you are searching out God's revelation—which is *not* off-limits to you. This is what I want you to understand today.

Some might use Scriptures like Isaiah 55:8-9 to make revelation seem inaccessible to you:

*"For My thoughts are not your thoughts, nor are your ways My ways," declares the Lord. "For as the heavens are higher than the earth, so are My ways higher than your ways and My thoughts than your thoughts."*

This Scripture is very true. At the same time, God was speaking to a people who were living in an Old Testament context. In other words, they were under the Old Covenant and were not yet accessible to the indwelling Spirit of God.

In Isaiah 64:4, we read another similar Scripture: "For from days of old they have not heard or perceived by ear, nor has the eye seen a God besides You, who acts in behalf of the one who waits for Him."

> **Meditation is you intently seeking God's revelation, resulting in God disclosing Himself to you.**

Both Old Testament passages make it sound like God's revelation is overly mysterious and inaccessible. Now, consider what the apostle Paul says in First Corinthians 2 and how the Holy Spirit radically changes the dynamic of hearing from God:

*But just as it is written, "Things which eye has not seen and ear has not heard, and which have not entered the heart of man, all that God has prepared for those who love Him." For to us God revealed them through the Spirit;*

*for the Spirit searches all things, even the depths of God* (1 Corinthians 2:9-10).

In the Old Covenant, the thoughts and ways of God were inaccessible; because of Jesus's work on the cross and the Holy Spirit, you now have the ability to know God's ways. You have the ability to hear His thoughts. This is what is taking place in biblical meditation—you are not just reading information. To approach Scripture this way is to take an Old Covenant posture, which we have been redeemed from. We have been brought into a relationship with the Author of Scripture, who, through the Holy Spirit, wants to disclose and reveal God to our spirit.

This is why Paul encouraged us to pray for the eyes of our hearts to be enlightened, so that we might *know* (Eph. 1:18).

## REFLECT

Explain the difference between the Old and New Covenant in terms of what kind of access people had to God. If Jesus's blood made it possible for you to hear God, and hear Him intimately and continuously, what kind of expectation should you be attaching to your time in the Scripture?

---

---

---

---

---

---

---

---

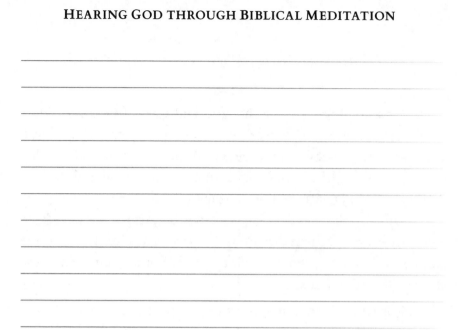

## DAILY SCRIPTURE MEDITATION

*But just as it is written, "Things which eye has not seen and ear has not heard, and which have not entered the heart of man, all that God has prepared for those who love Him." For to us God revealed them through the Spirit; for the Spirit searches all things, even the depths of God* (1 Corinthians 2:9-10).

## MEDITATION PROMPTS

- What do these Scriptures reveal about your ability to hear from God in the New Covenant (versus the Old)?

- How does the Holy Spirit living inside of you give you new levels of access to God's voice?

- Paul writes that the Spirit searches *even the depths of God.* What does this say about *what* kind of revelation you are able to hear from and about God?

# FOUR UNDERLYING PILLARS OF MEDITATION

The four underlying pillars of meditation are: 1) continuous activity, 2) God's Spirit utilizing every faculty of one's heart and mind, 3) results in revelation, and 4) revelation brings transformation.

Meditation is a *continuous* activity. We meditate everywhere—in bed, in the field, in the temple, and while working. We meditate all the time—day, evening, and nighttime. Meditation is our lifestyle (Phil. 4:8). We meditate on God and the things that are of Him—His splendor, His Majesty, His beauty, His Word, His precepts, His statutes, His ways, His works (i.e. His creation, the world), His activities (the things He does). We do not meditate on evil, wickedness, or the works of satan.

Meditation involves *God's Spirit utilizing every faculty* of one's heart and mind. Meditation is God's Spirit in our hearts guiding every faculty in both hemispheres of our brain (see diagram in Appendix A). We quiet down, using soft and/or instrumental music and/or seeing ourselves present with Him (Acts 2:25), and we sing, pray, seek, inquire (including taking our complaints to God to receive

His counsel). We speak, talk, mutter, communicate, babble (probably speaking in tongues), roar (at the enemy and when revelation hits), mourn (repent of our sins and mourn over the lost), muse, consider, ponder, imagine, study (study is good when wrapped with these other aspects of meditation). We sense the indwelling Holy Spirit crying out for intimacy with the Father (Gal. 4:6). See Appendix B for extended definitions of the word *meditate* from Hebrew and Greek dictionaries.

Meditation results in *revelation*. We quiet ourselves down in worship and prayer, asking for revelation (Eph. 1:17-18) while fixing our eyes on the Lord (Acts 2:25) who reveals truth to our hearts. We tune to flowing thoughts, visions, emotions, and power from the Holy Spirit within us (John 7:37–39). We experience our hearts burning with revelations as He opens Scriptures to us (Luke 24:15–32). His spoken word is powerful (Isa. 55:11; John 6:63).

Finally, revelation brings *transformation*! Burning revelation creates living truth in our hearts. We say, "Yes, Lord" to these revelations, coming into agreement with what we see Jesus doing and speaking. This results in us being transformed while we look at Jesus in action (2 Cor. 3:18; 4:17-18). These transformational moments occur continuously if we meditate.

I encourage you, engage the meditation journey daily so that you would become the radiant expression of Jesus and make your way prosperous (Heb. 12:2; Josh. 1:8).

# REFLECT

Which of the four pillars of meditation do you have the most questions about? I encourage you to begin meditating about that pillar of meditation right now. Let that be a starting point for your journey. Ask the Holy Spirit to give you insight into the process as you set out to start approaching Scripture with biblical meditation.

Visit some of the verses that I referenced, write them down, and invite the Spirit of God to grant you understanding into each pillar and how it's key for you to engage the process of biblical meditation.

You can use the space below for your thoughts and journaling.

# DAILY SCRIPTURE MEDITATION

*Finally, brethren, whatever is true, whatever is honorable, whatever is right, whatever is pure, whatever is lovely, whatever is of good repute, if there is any excellence and if anything worthy of praise, dwell on these things* (Philippians 4:8).

# MEDITATION PROMPTS

- How can Paul's list in Philippians 4:8 give you a blueprint for *what* you should be meditating on?

- How can this list help you evaluate what thoughts are godly and what thoughts should be rejected?

- Do a study on the word *dwell* in this passage. What does this mean and how does it relate to biblical meditation?

# Seven Steps to Receive Revelation Knowledge through Meditation

Revelation is not intended to sound like some overly mystical experience, nor should it be regarded as an un-biblical concept. With revelation, you are not *adding* to the canon of Scripture, as some mistakenly assume; instead, you are asking the Holy Spirit to unveil that which is under the surface. In other words, you are not looking outside of the Bible for revelation. You are coming to the Scripture, now aided by the most capable tutor imaginable—the Holy Spirit—and you are asking Him to shine light on what that passage means and how it can be applied.

An example of revelation knowledge is when you are reading the Bible and a verse leaps off the page, hits you between the eyes, and God says, *This is for you...right now!* These are precious experiences for the believer. However, for many they do not happen often enough.

 BIBLICAL MEDITATION

*"Results in illumination, revelation knowledge, and anointed reasoning."*

There are seven things I do which allow me the privilege of receiving revelation knowledge every time I read the Bible. Truth and insights leap off the page, and an understanding of how they are to adjust my life permeates my spirit and soul. I love this experience and hunger for it every time I read the Scriptures. That is why I prepare myself by doing the following seven things.

In this section, I am going to be as practical as possible. There are certain things that are *not* conducive to meditation, and likewise there are seven key practices that will help foster an environment fit for biblical meditation and, ultimately, the reception of revelation. Prayerfully reflect on these steps and determine which ones you do and don't use:

## DO *NOT* DO THIS:

(Left brain; study/rational humanism)

1. Have unconfessed sin

2. Have a preconceived attitude

3. Be independent: "I can…"

4. Read quickly

5. Rely on reason and analysis only

6. Read without specific purpose

7. Take credit for insights

# DO THIS INSTEAD:

(Whole brain/heart; meditation/divine revelation)

1. **Be washed by Jesus's blood.** *Lord, cleanse me by Your blood.* Because receiving divine revelation is at the heart of biblical meditation, you must prepare yourself to receive from the Holy Spirit by repenting and being cleansed by the blood of the Lamb. You must be obedient to previous revelations from God (Matt. 7:6) and confess any sin in your life, so you are not cut off from ongoing revelation (Isa. 59:1-2; 1 John 1:9).

2. **Have a teachable attitude.** *Lord, grant me a teachable attitude.* Revelation is given to those who maintain an attitude of humility, and it is withheld from the proud and the arrogant. So keep an open, humble attitude before God, allowing Him the freedom to shed greater light on any ideas you currently hold and to alter them as He sees fit (James 4:6; 2 Pet. 1:19).

3. **Yield.** *Lord, I will not use my faculties myself.* You can do nothing of your own initiative but only what you hear and see by the Spirit (John 5:19-20,30). You do not have a mind to use, but a mind to present to God so He can use it and fill it with anointed reason and divine vision (Prov. 3:5–7; Rom. 12:1-2). If you use your mind yourself, it is a dead work (Heb. 6:1-2).

4. **Pray.** *Lord, I pray that the eyes of my heart might be enlightened.* Slow down as you read, mulling the text over and over in your heart and mind, praying constantly for God to give you a spirit of wisdom and revelation in the knowledge of Him (Eph. 1:17-18; Ps. 119:18).

5. **Combine anointed reason, flowing pictures, music and speech.** *Lord, I present the abilities to reason and to imagine to You to fill and flow through by Your Spirit.* Meditation involves presenting your faculties to God for Him to fill and use. These include your left-brain reasoning capacities as well as your right-brain visual capacities. Look for the river of God (i.e. "Spirit flow") to guide and fill both hemispheres, granting you anointed reasoning and dreams and visions (John 7:37–39). Music can assist you, as can muttering, speaking, and writing as you go through the discovery process (2 Kings 3:15).

6. **Read with focused purpose.** *Lord, show me the solution to the problem I am facing.* Focused attention brings additional energies of concentration of heart and mind, which help release revelation. For example, note the difference between a ray of sunlight hitting a piece of paper and sunlight going through a magnifying glass to hit a piece of paper. The focused energy creates a ray so concentrated that the paper bursts into flames. When you have a hunger to master a new understanding and discipline, that hungry and searching heart will cause you to see things you would not normally see (Matt. 5:6).

7. **Glorify God for insights.** *Thank You, Lord, for what You have shown me.* Realizing that the revelation came from the indwelling Holy Spirit, give all the glory to God for what has been revealed (Eph. 3:21).

## REFLECT

Write down your understanding of what biblical revelation is and what it looks like when you receive it. (Remember, it is important that you are able to clearly define this, as revelation is one of the key objectives of biblical meditation.)

_____
_____
_____
_____
_____
_____
_____
_____
_____
_____
_____
_____

## DAILY SCRIPTURE MEDITATION

*One thing I have asked from the Lord, that I shall seek: that I may dwell in the house of the Lord all the days of my life, to behold the beauty of the Lord and to meditate in His temple* (Psalm 27:4).

## MEDITATION PROMPTS

- Go back and review the seven-step process to receiving revelation.

- Use this process as you approach today's Scripture meditation in Psalm 27.

- Document your experience using the seven-step process, writing down the revelation you receive about this passage.

# *Part Two*

# How to Encounter
# God in the Bible

*My eyes anticipate the night watches, that
I may meditate on Your word.*
—Psalm 119:148

*Prayer that is born of meditation upon the
Word of God is the prayer that soars upward
most easily to God's listening ears.*
—R.A. Torrey

*Chapter 6*

# How to Handle the Bible Properly

Here is a quick, twelve-point guide to properly handling Scripture as you approach the meditation process. This is absolutely worth noting due to the amount of confusion and misunderstanding surrounding the subject of biblical meditation.

1. *The Scriptures are authoritative, infallible, and universal* in their application for humanity (2 Tim. 3:16).

2. *The Bible is alive* (Heb. 4:12) and thus must be interpreted as a living, active force, not plain text. This includes the realization that its words have the spiritual energy to change us. (In Hebrews 4:12 the word translated "active" is *energes* and means "active energy.") The Spirit reveals specific truths from each verse at each point in our lives. Each passage contains many emphases that the Spirit can bring forth.

3. Truth is *progressive* in nature. For example, in the Old Testament you were unclean if you touched a leper

(Lev. 22:4-5); however, in the New Testament Jesus touched lepers and they became clean (Mark 1:40-41). An Old Testament law remains intact unless Jesus fulfilled or changed it.

4.  I must be *wholehearted* in my search if I want God to disclose Himself to me (1 Chron. 28:9; Jer. 29:13; Prov. 8:17; Matt. 5:6).

5.  I must have a *pure heart* if I want to *see God* (Matt. 5:8; 1 Cor. 13:13; Titus 1:15-16; Heb. 10:19–22). The Bible is veiled until one turns to the Lord and the Spirit enters and the *veil is taken away*, and we *see* clearly, being transformed by that which we are seeing (2 Cor. 3:15–17).

6.  Truth is *"Presence" driven* (Ps. 73:16-17) rather than principle driven. Jesus lived out of the voice and vision of the Father (John 5:19-20,30). The Pharisees lived out of biblical laws. The new wineskin that doesn't break is the one that is kept elastic by the oil of the Holy Spirit (Gal. 3:3).

7.  *The Holy Spirit has the final say-so* on the meaning of Scripture, as He is its author (John 16:13; Luke 24:32; John 6:63; Rom. 8:6,14; 1 Cor. 2:10–16; 2 Cor. 3:6; Gal. 5:18).

8.  *The Spirit continues* to speak authoritatively to us *today* (Acts 2:17; John 16:13).

9.  *Careful, Spirit-led observation* of biblical texts can reveal God's original intentions. Luke 1:1–3 shows careful observation that was guided by the Spirit (2 Tim. 3:16).

10. I must *act upon* the revelation God gives if I want more revelation (James 1:22–27; Rom. 8:13; Gal. 5:25).

11. Truth is discovered within the *context of community* (2 Cor. 13:1; Acts 15; Prov. 11:14).

12. Truth is vindicated by her *deeds*. Truth produces good fruit (Matt. 11:19; 7:16; Gal. 5:6,22; 1 Tim. 1:3–5; 1 John 2:9; 1 Cor. 4:12–16; 1 Tim. 6:3–6; Col. 3:15; Rom. 14:17; 2 Cor. 7:1; Eph. 2:1–7; 4:3,17–25; 1 Pet. 3:8–11; Jude 1:19; Heb. 10:24–29).

## REFLECT

One common theme in these 12 steps is the emphasis on the Holy Spirit. Why is it so important that you approach the Scripture under the Spirit's influence and instruction, rather than just using your natural human reasoning?

_____

_____

_____

_____

_____

_____

_____

_____

_____

_____

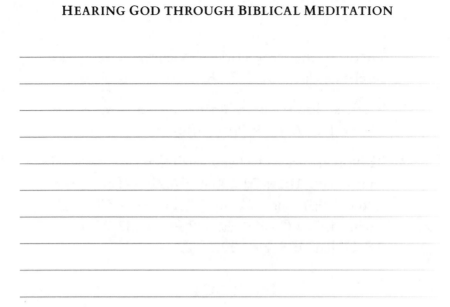

## DAILY SCRIPTURE MEDITATION

*O how I love Your law! It is my meditation all the day* (Psalm 119:97).

## MEDITATION PROMPTS

- Explain how you think it would be possible to meditate on the Word of God *all the day*, as the psalmist writes.

- Write down some practical ways you can continuously keep the Scriptures in front of your mind's eye.

- What do you think the psalmist means when he writes, "O how I *love* Your law!" Explain what it looks like to love the Word of God.

## IMPARTATION PRAYER

As you continue on this journey to discovering and practicing biblical meditation, I want your prayer to be just like the psalmist's: *O how I love Your law*!

You can pray with me:

*Father, I ask You to give me a fresh love and delight for Your Word.*

*Holy Spirit, I give You complete control of the meditation process. You are completely trustworthy, so I trust You to be my tutor, my guide, my instructor, and my partner in this journey.*

*For what I don't understand about biblical meditation, I ask You to come and bring clarity.*

*Open the Scriptures to me so that words on a page come to life. Thank You, Lord, that I can expect revelation that produces transformation in every area of my life.*

*In Jesus's name,*

*Amen!*

*Chapter 7*

# Basic Principles for Interpreting Scripture

In preparing you to fully engage the biblical meditation process, I want to give you some basic principles of hermeneutics (keys to interpreting Scripture properly). This will prove to be a handy list that you can refer to often when approaching the Scriptures.

1.  You must understand the similarities and differences between the Old and New Testaments. The similarities are much greater and more vital than the differences. The New Testament grows out of, and is in many ways a continuation of, the Old Testament.

2.  However the New Testament interprets an Old Testament verse is to be accepted as the correct interpretation.

3.  No doctrine should be founded on a single passage (John 5:31–39; 8:16–18).

4.  No important doctrine should be based alone on a type, figurative expression, or parable, but rather on plain and literal stories and teachings, allowing the former to illustrate the truth.

5.  Decide whether the verse is universal in its application or limited to those to whom it was initially addressed. The context and other teaching on the topic should make it clear whether it is limited or universal. Do not presuppose any limits on Scripture that are not *clearly taught* in the Word of God.

6.  Scripture should be used to interpret Scripture. Brief statements are to be interpreted by fuller ones.

7.  The whole counsel of God concerning a subject is found by collecting and correlating all verses on that subject, attempting to see *all* sides of the truth.

8.  Although, generally speaking, Scripture is to be taken in its plain, simple, literal meaning, you should realize there is some non-literal language in the Bible. A rule of thumb to help you discern literal from non-literal is to take words in their literal sense when given their plain and natural settings, and figuratively when the word is joined to an object to which it does not normally or naturally belong (e.g., Matt. 23:24).

9.  You must properly recognize and interpret types. A type is a person or thing in the Old Testament that was divinely designed to be a foreshadowing of a person or thing in the New Testament. Those things taught to be types by the New Testament are definitely types. However, in going beyond that to your own speculation you are on unsure ground. (Examples of

types are found in Exodus 12:1–28; John 1:29; First Corinthians 5:6-7; and 1 Peter 1:9–19.)

10. When interpreting parables you should: a) find the basic point the parable was meant to make; b) realize that every other point of the parable does not necessarily have an applied meaning (or else in Luke 18:1–8, God would be considered the unjust judge); c) realize a parable only illustrates a subject *partially*; and d) understand that parables are designed to illustrate, not to teach directly.

11. Use the **Law of Relationship**: Everything written or spoken sustains some specific relationship to something else. It may be in conduct, repetition, cause and effect, means to an end, or some other relationship. We must consider these relationships to order our thought processes in light of the passage.

12. Use the **Law of Proportion**: An author reveals his emphasis, or lack of it, by the relative amount of treatment given to a specific subject. He may emphasize or omit certain parts completely, depending on how they relate to his development of thought. Examine people, places, time, events, and ideas.

13. Use the **Law of First Mention**, which states that because God knows the end from the beginning, the first mention of a subject in Scripture will have in it the basic elements of that subject as it is further developed in Scripture. For example, trace the theme of the heart starting from Genesis 6:5.

14. Include all aspects of meditation as it was originally understood in Scripture rather than limiting yourself to mere intellectual study.

# REFLECT

Why do you think it is so important for you to have a correct interpretation of Scripture while engaging the biblical meditation process?

_____

_____

_____

_____

_____

_____

_____

_____

_____

_____

_____

_____

_____

_____

_____

_____

_____

_____

## DAILY SCRIPTURE MEDITATION

_Do your best to present yourself to God as one approved, a worker who has no need to be ashamed, rightly handling the word of truth_ (2 Timothy 2:15 ESV).

## MEDITATION PROMPTS

- How do the 14 principles for interpreting Scripture help you _rightly handle_ the word of truth?

- Why do you think that _rightly handling the word of truth_ makes someone a worker "who has no need to be ashamed"?

# How Is the Old Testament Relevant for Your Life Today?

The Old Testament is especially relevant for your life today and, thus, should be meditated upon. Paul notes that what was written in the Old Testament—specifically, the things that happened to the children of Israel—was written for our instruction.

What happened to Israel happened as an example for us and was written for our instruction so that we would not make the same mistakes and fall (1 Cor. 10:11-12).

Also, we see that many things in the Old Testament are copies, shadows, or types of the spiritual things we find in the New Testament and, as such, help us in understanding the New Testament (Heb. 8:5).

Finally, the Old Testament is relevant to us today because our faith is built up as we meditate on the provision of God for His people and the promises He made to them, while realizing that all these promises are reaffirmed in Christ to us, because He has given us an

even better covenant which has been enacted on better promises
(2 Cor. 1:20; Heb. 8:6).

# REFLECT

Why do you think it's important for you to study the Old Testament, even though Jesus has redeemed you and made you an
inheritor of the New Covenant?

_____

_____

_____

_____

_____

_____

_____

_____

_____

_____

_____

_____

_____

_____

_____

_____

_____

_____

_____

_____

_____

_____

_____

In the modern church, there is often the tendency to bypass the Old Testament, exclusively focusing on the New.

Take a moment right now to think of some *key stories and figures in the Old Testament that you would like to study*. Write these down and be intentional about spending time in these portions of Scripture. Most importantly, ask the Holy Spirit to direct your focus.

_____

_____

_____

_____

_____

_____

_____

_____

_____

_____

_____

_____

_____

_____

_____

_____

_____

_____

_____

_____

_____

_____

_____

_____

## DAILY SCRIPTURE MEDITATION

_Now these things happened to them as an example, and they were written for our instruction, upon whom the ends of the ages have come_ (1 Corinthians 10:11).

## MEDITATION PROMPTS

- Consider the full context of First Corinthians 10. (You might wish to read the entire chapter.)

- How can studying the Old Testament stories _protect_ you from falling into the same traps and mistakes as the children of Israel?

- How can studying the Old Testament build your faith in God's supernatural provision and miracle-working power?

# Chapter 9

# WHAT IS INVOLVED IN CAREFUL, SPIRIT–LED OBSERVATION OF A BIBLE STORY?

The stories recorded in the Bible reveal to us the love of God toward the entire world and toward us individually. They reveal the sovereignty of a God who rules over the realm of mankind, working all things according to the counsel of His will. They reveal the exceeding great and precious promises that have been given to us in Christ. They instruct us in the way we can live as the Creator intended—in peace and contentment. They are examples for us that encourage us to have our own similar encounters with Almighty God.

Having a strong, deep knowledge of the whole counsel of God as revealed in the Scriptures provides a solid foundation upon which to build one's life. Treasuring the Word of God in your heart is a safeguard against sin. By no means do we minimize the importance of applying yourself to knowing the Scriptures. Rather, we passionately desire that you do not stop with gaining an intellectual understanding and analysis. Even unbelievers can do that.

> Treasuring the Word of God in your heart is a safeguard against sin.

Do your study and research and analysis and examination, always following the leading of the Spirit. Then take the next steps—give Him the opportunity to speak directly to you about what you read, and respond in every appropriate way.

## REFLECT

Write down your idea of what it means to be *Spirit-led* when it comes to studying the Scriptures.

_____

_____

_____

_____

_____

_____

_____

_____

_____

_____

_____

_____

_____

_____

_____

_____

_____

_____

_____

_____

How can be it be dangerous if you only approach the Bible through analysis, study, and research *without* the illuminating aid of the Holy Spirit?

_____

_____

_____

_____

_____

_____

_____

_____

_____

_____

_____

_____

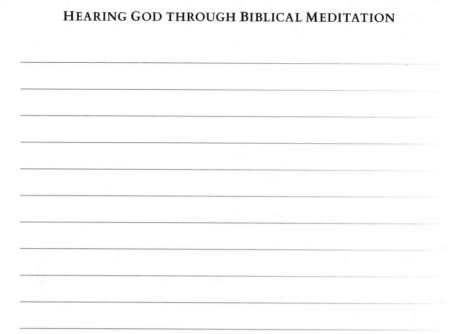

## DAILY SCRIPTURE MEDITATION

*For whatever was written in earlier times was written for our instruction, so that through perseverance and the encouragement of the Scriptures we might have hope* (Romans 15:4).

## MEDITATION PROMPTS

- How does the Word of God provide practical instruction to your everyday life?

- Describe how meditating upon certain stories in the Bible can strengthen your perseverance as you approach difficult circumstances in your life.

- How can the encouragement of the Scriptures give you hope (even when, like Abraham—who believed for his miracle child, Isaac—there is no logical or natural reason to be filled with hope)?

# KEYS FOR INDUCTIVE BIBLE STUDY

In this segment, I want to give you a few practical keys to approaching Bible study inductively. We must always begin with a hunger for God's truth, not our truth. We banish fear, pride, and prejudice, and come into His presence to hear from God and receive from Him.

The key to good interpretation of biblical texts is to learn to read the text carefully and to ask the right questions of the text.

Use the disciplines of inductive Bible study, which are:

1.  prayer

2.  observation,

3.  interpretation

4.  application

## STEP 1: PRAYER

*Holy Spirit, I ask You to give me wisdom and understanding of the Scripture.*

Ask the Holy Spirit to give you wisdom and understanding of the text (John 16:13–15; Prov. 2:1–10; Eph. 1:17-18), and then listen to Him in observation, interpretation, and application, which means you tune in to His flowing thoughts, pictures, and emotions (John 7:37–39).

Prayer is essential because you are recognizing that, from the very outset of the process of biblical meditation, the Holy Spirit is not only involved—He is the One steering and directing it.

## STEP 2: OBSERVATION

*Holy Spirit, help me observe the characters and key themes in this passage.*

Ask the following questions about what is going on in the passage of Scripture:

1. **Who** is speaking? Who is this about? Who are the main characters? To whom is God speaking?

2. **What** is the subject or event covered in the chapter? What do you learn about the people, event, or teaching?

3. **When** do/will the events occur or when did/will something happen to someone in particular?

4. **Where** did/will this happen? Where was it said?

5. **Why** is something being said or mentioned? Why would/will this happen? Why at that time and/or to this person/people?

6. **How** will it happen? How is it to be done? How is it illustrated?

7. **Relationship with God and others**: The Bible is a history of God relating Himself to humanity, His

relationship with them, and their relationship with Him and with others among His people:

- Lord, what does this passage reveal *about You* and Your heart toward me? How can this be put in terms that a child, a young person, or an adult can understand?

- Lord, what does the passage show *about people*? How can this be put in terms a child, a young person, or an adult can understand?

- Lord, what are the themes and elements central to what the passage shows *about You interacting with mankind and mankind interacting with You*? How does this change the way we interact with one another?

- Lord, what are the deeper issues in the passage which will help me to *experience You and release Your grace to others*? What dynamic or principle in this passage helps me grow into a closer walk with Jesus?

## STEP 3:  INTERPRETATION

Interpretation answers the question, "What does the passage mean?"

*Holy Spirit, show me what this passage meant to the biblical audience and what it means to me today.*

*Context always rules first* (2 Pet. 3:15-16). Never take a Scripture out of its context to make it say what you want it to say. Look at context first from the perspective of the book being studied, the overall chapter, the paragraph, and the sentence. Try to stay away from giving individual words meanings that reinterpret sentences, paragraphs, etc.

*Always seek the full counsel of God's Word* (2 Pet. 3:15-16). Never accept someone's teaching based on one or two verses; ensure that they're not taken out of context as they are employed throughout the whole Bible. The interpretation that is the best interpretation is that which accounts for the broadest range of relevant evidence. If someone claims that one particular passage's content shows that the Bible teaches "thus and so" without explaining the ten other passages that convey a different perspective on the same teaching, that author has not adequately explained all the relevant evidence.

*Scripture never contradicts Scripture.* "Believe in *all* that the prophets have spoken" (Luke 24:25). The best interpreter of Scripture is the Lord leading us to other thematically related Scriptures. One of the best study aids is a good Bible dictionary that will show words and concepts as they are presented throughout *all* of Scripture. This is often the best use of footnotes in your Bible that indicate other verses utilizing the same words or phrases in other places so you can compare and contrast how it is used in many passages.

*Use the Seven Steps of Biblical Meditation* as described later in this book.

## STEP 4: APPLICATION

Application answers the question: Lord, what does this mean to me personally? What truths can I put into practice? What changes do You want to make to my life?

Throughout the process of biblical study, interpretation, and meditation you should do the following:

- Receive input from your spiritual advisors

- Check for peace in your heart

- Make sure that the fruit of your interpretation bears life as you apply the insights in real time

Evangelist D.L. Moody explained: "When we find a man meditating on the words of God, my friends, that man is full of boldness and is successful." Application of our biblical meditation produces transformation. Moody noted that boldness and good success (just as the Lord promised to Joshua) are just two of the by-products of putting biblical meditation to practice in our lives.

*Part Three*

# WHAT IS BIBLICAL MEDITATION?

*Open my eyes so that I may contemplate
wonderful things from Your instruction.*
—PSALM 119:18 HCSB

*The more you read the Bible; and the more you meditate
on it, the more you will be astonished with it.*
—CHARLES SPURGEON

 **BIBLICAL MEDITATION**

**"God's Spirit utilizing every faculty of my heart and mind,
bringing forth revelation which ushers in transformation."**

# A Real-Life Example of Meditation from Second Corinthians 3:18

## Dr. Mark Virkler

I would like to share just one example of the transforming impact that biblical meditation has had in my life. I received the following revelation as I meditated on this Scripture:

> But we all, with unveiled face, **beholding** as in a mirror **the glory of the Lord**, are **being transformed** into the same image from glory to glory (Second Corinthians 3:18).

I fought to *be transformed* in several areas of my life. I did not like the sin that I saw in my life in these areas, and even though I focused intently on overcoming the sin, I was not able to get rid of it. All I felt was guilt, condemnation, and despair as I said, "Lord, I cannot overcome this sin no matter what I do."

So as I prayerfully meditated on the above Scripture, I asked, "Lord, what do You mean that we are transformed as we *behold the glory of the Lord*? I *behold* the misery of my sin and I am not experiencing anything other than condemnation. You have clearly said there is no condemnation to those who are in Christ. Aren't I in You?"

*What is my problem?*

Then the Lord spoke during my journaling time.

> *Mark, whatever you focus on grows within you, and whatever grows within you, you become. Focus on Me and My glory, and you will be transformed into My likeness. You become a reflection of that which you gaze upon.*

Wow! So I don't gaze at my sin, my weakness and inability to overcome it, or the biblical laws that tell me not to do it. Instead, I focus on Him! What an insight. I had been focusing in all the wrong places. When I focused on my sin, sinfulness grew within me and I became a bigger sinner. When I focused on biblical law, law grew within me and I became a legalist. When I focused on my weakness to keep the law, guilt and condemnation grew within me and I became depressed.

Now it is clear that I am to fix my eyes on Jesus (Acts 2:25; Heb. 12:1-2) and Jesus grows within me. *Can I roar this from the hilltops?* All my life I have practiced Christianity wrong! The results of my wrong practicing were not positive; they produced guilt, condemnation, and death. Now, in a flash of revelation, which I received as a result of prayerfully meditating on Scripture, I saw the light—I am to fix my eyes on Jesus, and Jesus grows within me and I become Christlike!

*This one revelation has transformed my entire approach to Christianity,* as well as my preaching and my writing style. Now I preach and write about *who Christ is within* the believer and how to tap in to His indwelling life. Everything changed in a blinding flash of revelation. My life was completely transformed. This is biblical meditation at work. This is what we want you, our reader, to experience.

ooooo

I have grown up in a world that knows nothing about biblical meditation. We know how to study, but we have never been taught how to meditate in a simple, childlike way.

When I read what the ancient Christian mystics did for meditation, I said, "That is too hard and impractical for my modern life." I just could not do what they did and still be engaged in society. And I sure do not want to disengage from society. Jesus didn't. He stayed involved. So can we make biblical meditation something simple enough and clear enough that we can do it while fully engaged in society and life?

The answer is "Yes, we can!" *This is what you will be discovering in this following segment as you learn how practical the art of biblical meditation really is.*

# BIBLICAL MEDITATION IS HOLY SPIRIT DIRECTED

In Appendix B, I will provide approximately 68 Scripture verses that deal with biblical meditation. Meditation is *the central way* that God wants us to approach the Bible.

Spirit-led study is one component of this meditation process. The activities listed in the following definitions of meditation are to be the things we do as we approach God through Scripture. Embrace these activities as you meditate on Scripture. They are summarized in the "Seven Steps of Biblical Meditation" in the next chapter. These steps will allow you to meditate God's way which produces Spirit life (John 6:63).

For now, I want to give you some working biblical definitions of the word *meditate*. The meanings of these six words (featured in Appendix B) include pray, mutter, speak, imagine, study, roar, mourn, ponder, revolve in the mind, and devotion. Because prayer and devotion are involved, it is God's Spirit guiding the meditation process granting insight, revelation, and ultimately spiritual transformation as we draw upon God's in-working power to implement the revelations being granted by His Holy Spirit.

Meditation is not self-directed; it is Spirit-directed. Throughout the process, God is in charge. This is the uniqueness of biblical meditation versus Eastern meditation or even our traditional concept of study.

Internationally known author and speaker Joyce Huggett makes it expressly clear that "Christian meditation must not be confused with yoga, Eastern meditation or transcendental meditation...Christian meditation has nothing to do with emptying our minds...[it] engages every part of us—our mind, our emotions, our imagination, our creativity, and supremely, our will."[1]

In Eastern meditation, the mind is emptied, thus opening one up to the influence of demonic spirits. With biblical meditation, from the very beginning the process is being placed under the most capable guidance of Holy Spirit. With traditional study, the natural human intellect is in control, directing the process.

With biblical meditation, we are inviting the Holy Spirit to take us into the Scriptures as only He can. Remember, Scripture is God-breathed, according to Paul:

> *All Scripture is God-breathed and is useful for teaching, rebuking, correcting and training in righteousness* (2 Timothy 3:16 NIV).

Even though the traditional language associated with this passage is "God-breathed," perhaps the more relevant expression would be "all Scripture is inspired by God" (NASB). Literally, what we recognize as Scripture was *breathed out* by God and given to us. Can you imagine the problems that result when we approach the Bible *without* the guidance of Holy Spirit?

I want you to really consider the implications of this. When you are meditating on the Scriptures—under the direction and influence of God's Holy Spirit—you are being personally taught by the very One who authored the Bible.

## REFLECT

What do you think it means to be Spirit-directed when it comes to biblical meditation? Why do you think it is so important for you to yield your mind and traditional study approaches to the leading and guidance of the Holy Spirit in the meditation process? Explain what this looks like and write/pray a prayer to the Spirit of God, asking Him to direct you in biblical meditation.

_____

_____

_____

_____

_____

_____

_____

_____

_____

_____

_____

_____

_____

_____

_____

_____

_____

_____

_____

_____

_____

_____

_____

_____

_____

_____

_____

## DAILY SCRIPTURE MEDITATION

*All Scripture is God-breathed and is useful for teaching, rebuking, correcting and training in righteousness* (2 Timothy 3:16 NIV).

## MEDITATION PROMPTS

- What does Paul mean when he describes Scripture as being "God-breathed"?

- If Scripture is God-inspired, why do you think it's so important to be directed by the Holy Spirit when you read it?

### NOTE

1. Richard Foster, ed., *Spiritual Classics: Selected Readings on the 12 Spiritual Disciplines* (New York: HarperOne, 2007), 10-11.

# THE ART OF SUCCESSFUL BIBLICAL MEDITATION

Before you begin to engage the meditation process, keep in mind that an interpreter of Scripture must have the following:

1.  A mind illumined by the Holy Spirit (Ps. 119:18,130; 1 Cor. 2:6–16; Eph. 1:17-18; James 1:5).

2.  A humble, teachable, unprejudiced heart and mind (Matt. 5:3,11–25; Luke 8:15; James 4:6).

3.  The right motive, which is to get better acquainted with God and His will for your life (2 Thess. 2:10; 1 Tim. 2:4; 2 Tim. 2:15; 3:1–9, especially verse 7).

If you want to encounter God through biblical meditation, your success hinges on the following:

*Your heart hungers and thirsts for God's truth* (Matt. 5:6), no matter what it costs (reputation, pride, ego, job, financial security, etc.).

*It is done while in the Lord's presence* (Ps. 73:16-17) through spiritual worship. Be humble and teachable, repenting of all sins, asking for and receiving the cleansing of His blood (Heb. 10:22) and putting on His robe of righteousness (Gal. 3:27) so His revelation can flow.

*You reason only with the Lord* and never apart from Him. "'Come now, and let us reason *together*,' says the Lord" (Isa. 1:18). Spirit-led reasoning is reasoning guided by the flow of His Spirit (John 7:37–39).

*You are wholehearted in your search* (Jer. 29:13) trusting in the Lord's revelation rather than your own human understanding when the two conflict. "Trust in the Lord with all your heart and do not lean on your own understanding. In all your ways acknowledge Him (interact with Him, Hebrew *yada*: "know, experience") and He will make your paths straight" (Prov. 3:5-6).

*You honor and seek input* from your spiritual advisors (Prov. 11:14; 2 Cor. 13:1).

You allow the *peace of God in your heart* to confirm you have arrived at truth (Col. 3:15).

And finally, you allow the *fruit it bears in your life* to confirm you have arrived at truth (Matt. 7:16).

## REFLECT

What do you think it looks like to read the Bible in the presence of God? How is this important when it comes to experiencing God through biblical meditation?

# DAILY SCRIPTURE MEDITATION

*When I pondered to understand this, it was troublesome in my sight until I came into the sanctuary of God; then I perceived their end* (Psalm 73:16-17).

# MEDITATION PROMPTS

- Read Psalm 73 in its entirety, getting a clear context for what David is referencing here in verses 16 and 17. He is talking about his enemies/the enemies of God.

- How does coming into the sanctuary/presence of God give us increased understanding?

- Based on these passages, why do you think it is so important to read/consider Scripture in the presence of God?

*Chapter 12*

# HOW TO MEDITATE ON A TOPIC

I want to give you seven steps to begin the meditation process. Immediately after reading this segment, I want you to *engage* an exercise where you will personally go through this meditation process.

1. *Be led by God to the topic*: God will show you the topic He wants you to explore, by bringing it to your consciousness through thoughts, the comment of a friend or a book, or a presenting need in your life that demands the revelation and power of God to overcome (John 16:13).

2. *Be cleansed by His blood*: Approach your meditation time by drawing near to the Lord, repenting of all sins and asking for and receiving the cleansing of His blood (Heb. 10:22).

3. *Be humble and teachable*: Ask for the Holy Spirit to reveal truth to you (Eph. 1:17-18). Be willing to discover

and embrace His truth, no matter what it costs (reputation, pride, ego, job, financial security, etc.).

4.   *Be fearless*: Some churches will excommunicate, fire, or shun a person who disagrees with the church's belief. Thus, fear hinders many from pursuing truth. Put your whole trust in God to sustain you, even if you are shunned or rejected by organized religion.

5.   *Be wholehearted in your search*: Seek the Lord with your whole heart (i.e. presenting all your faculties to the Lord to fill and to use) and you will find Him (Jer. 29:13). Ask the Holy Spirit to guide and fill your heart and then tune to flowing thoughts, flowing pictures, flowing emotions.

6.   *Let the Holy Spirit guide you* in the use of the following Bible tools:

- A good concordance such as *Strong's Exhaustive Concordance* and the *King James Concordance* (gives you every verse where a specific Hebrew or Greek word is used).

- Some good Bible dictionaries such as *Strong's Complete Dictionary of Bible Words, Brown-Driver-Briggs Hebrew and English Lexicon, Vine's Complete Expository Dictionary of Old and New Testament Words*.

- Miscellaneous analytical tools such as *Nave's Topical Bible* and *Manners and Customs of the Bible*, etc.

- Interpretive tools such as exegetical commentaries, expository commentaries, and devotional commentaries.

7. *Receive counsel*: Wisdom and safety come from receiving counsel, input, and confirmation from the five-fold team God has given to you (Prov. 11:14; Eph. 4:11; 2 Cor. 13:1).

Most of the above tools (plus many more) are available electronically in the free software e-Sword. Our online college course, Biblical Research Methods from Christian Leadership University, also provides excellent training on how to research a topic using these tools.

## EXERCISE

Instead of doing a reflection/meditation scripture today, I want you to engage each of the seven steps listed in this segment. The goal of this entire book is not to simply provide you with information and instruction *about* meditation; instead, I want to personally take you through the process of biblical meditation so that you can experience the life-changing revelation that it brings about.

Step 1: *Ask the Holy Spirit to lead you to a topic.* Too often, we over-spiritualize this step. Simply take a moment to consider any of the thoughts, ideas, or presenting needs that come into your mind. It is highly recommended that you focus on a topic that is *relevant* to your everyday life. Doctrine and theology are necessary, but the whole point of learning truth is so we can put it into practice in our lives so that it can bear the fruit that Jesus promised it would.

Write down the topic/portion of Scripture that He leads you to:

_____

_____

_____

_____

_____

_____

_____

_____

_____

_____

_____

_____

_____

_____

_____

_____

_____

_____

_____

_____

_____

_____

_____

_____

_____

_____

Step 2: *Receive the cleansing of Jesus's blood.* The enemy will want to deceive you right out of enjoying God in this time of meditation. He has intentionally fought against biblical meditation because he is well aware of the breakthrough, victory, joy, and fulfillment it brings into our lives—ultimately drawing us closer to the heart and purposes of God.

Take this moment to:

- Repent of your sin.

- Receive the cleansing that Jesus provided through His blood.

- Realize that because of Jesus's blood, you are in right standing with God, fit to enter His presence and worthy to hear His voice.

Step 3: *Approach this time with humility and ask the Holy Spirit to teach you.* Humility is a key step in the process of biblical meditation, because we are literally laying down the supremacy of our study methods and surrendering to the Spirit's guidance through the process. Simply pray right now and ask the Holy Spirit to lead the process of biblical meditation, entrusting yourself to Him.

Step 4: *Be fearless.* Some Christians struggle with Step 3 because they are afraid that the process of biblical meditation will open them up to demonic or evil spirits. This is a lie when you are willfully and intentionally giving the process over to the Holy Spirit. Don't fear! Remember what Jesus said:

> *Now suppose one of you fathers is asked by his son for a fish; he will not give him a snake instead of a fish, will he? Or if he is asked for an egg, he will not give him a scorpion, will he? If you then, being evil, know how to give good gifts to your children, how much more will your heavenly Father give the Holy Spirit to those who ask Him?* (Luke 11:11–13)

*When you yield to the Holy Spirit, God will not allow anything evil to come enter you.*

Step 5: *Seek the Lord with your whole heart.* Approach the Scripture with expectation, confident that you will not just read *about* God in this time; you will actually experience Him! The Lord promised: "You will seek Me and find Me when you search for Me with all your heart" (Jer. 29:13).

Seek the Lord with your whole heart (presenting all your faculties to the Lord to fill and to use) and you will find Him. Ask the Holy Spirit to guide and fill your heart and then tune to flowing thoughts, flowing pictures, flowing emotions.

Step 6: *Let the Holy Spirit guide you* in the use of the Bible tools mentioned above.

Step 7: *Receive counsel.* Wisdom and safety come from receiving counsel, input, and confirmation from the fivefold team God has given to you (Prov. 11:14; Eph. 4:11; 2 Cor. 13:1).

Chapter 13

# How Study and Meditation Work Together

While we are not looking to study as the key vehicle through which we approach the Bible, study is nevertheless a vital component of meditation.

Remember, study is one part of the meditation process. In the case of Spirit-led study, it is the flow of the Spirit within man that guides him in what to search, where to focus, what questions to ask, what resources to turn to, and helps him discern the truth.

A Bible passage does have a basic meaning that can be discovered by the text, context, culture, intent of the writer, and God's intent. To discover this basic meaning you would use the principles of inductive Bible study. As you continue to meditate upon the passage, God deepens the revelation within your heart and mind and personalizes it to your situation. He wants to speak directly to the need in your life today, and He will do so through the process of biblical meditation.

When Romans 12:2 says to be transformed by the renewing of your mind, the transliterated Greek word for "mind" is *nous*, which is probably from the base of *ginosko*. *Ginosko* means to know through personal experience and is the word also used to describe sexual intimacy. This is a "knowing" that embraces spiritual intimacy and revelation knowledge from the heart, and it is much more than simple rational comprehension. The renewing of our minds that leads to the transformation of our lives is not merely an increased intellectual knowledge of theology and the Scriptures, but rather experiencing an intimate relationship with God and His Word.

Bill Johnson has made the insightful and incredibly important observation that God did not reveal Himself to Abraham as Jehovah Jireh to increase his knowledge or understanding of theology. Rather, God revealed Himself as Jehovah Jireh because He wanted Abraham to *experience* Him as the One who provides for all his needs.

I love this quote from Bill: "It's hard to have the same fruit as the early church when we value a book they didn't have above the Holy Spirit they did have."

When you add to "study" *all* of the steps of biblical meditation, you are allowing the living, ever present, Almighty God an opportunity to speak a fresh *rhema* word directly to your heart which can be:

1. **A re-affirmation or application of the original message.** Here are examples of literal New Testament fulfillment of Old Testament Scriptures:

   - Matthew 1:23 with Isaiah 7:14
   - Acts 13:23 with Isaiah 11:1
   - Matthew 21:42 with Isaiah 28:16 and Psalm 118:22
   - Luke 3:4–6 with Isaiah 40:3–5
   - Matthew 3:16-17 and 17:5 with Isaiah 42:1
   - Matthew 26:67 and 27:26,30 with Isaiah 50:6

- John 12:37-38 with Isaiah 53:1
- Acts 8:32-33 with Isaiah 53:7-8
- Matthew 26:63 and 27:12,14 with Isaiah 53:7
- John 1:29 with Isaiah 53:7
- First Peter 2:22 with Isaiah 53:9
- Luke 22:37 with Isaiah 53:12
- Luke 4:18-19 with Isaiah 61:1-2
- Matthew 21:5 with Isaiah 62:11 and Zechariah 9:9

2. **An expansion or alternative spiritual adaption of the original message.** Here are examples of the New Testament changing the meaning of an Old Testament verse:

- Luke 20:17-18 with Isaiah 8:14-15
- Hebrews 2:13 with Isaiah 8:17-18
- Matthew 4:12–16 with Isaiah 9:1-2
- John 4:10,14 with Isaiah 12:3
- First Corinthians 15:54 with Isaiah 25:8
- First Corinthians 14:21-22 with Isaiah 28:11
- Matthew 11:5 with Isaiah 29:18 and 35:5
- Hebrews 8:6,10–12 with Isaiah 42:6
- Matthew 11:5 and Luke 4:18 with Isaiah 42:7
- Acts 13:47 with Isaiah 49:6
- Matthew 8:16-17 with Isaiah 53:4
- John 6:45 with Isaiah 54:13
- Romans 10:20 with Isaiah 65:1
- Matthew 2:15 with Hosea 11:1

- Romans 3:10–18 with Psalm 5:9; 10:7; 14:1–3; 36:1; 53:1–3; 140:3; Proverbs 1:16; Ecclesiastes 7:20; Isaiah 59:7-8

# REFLECT

Take some time to explain the difference between study and meditation. This would be an excellent time to refer to Appendix C, where we have provided a contrast of these two practices.

Describe what intellectual study looks like:

_____

_____

_____

_____

_____

_____

_____

_____

_____

_____

_____

_____

_____

_____

_____

_____

Describe what biblical meditation looks like:

Explain the difference between the two practices in your own words:

_____

_____

_____

_____

_____

_____

_____

_____

_____

_____

_____

_____

_____

_____

_____

_____

_____

_____

_____

_____

_____

# DAILY SCRIPTURE MEDITATION

*And do not be conformed to this world, but be transformed by the renewing of your mind* (Greek for mind is *nous*, coming from *ginosko* which is a word for intimacy, thus "intimate knowledge"), *so that you may prove what the will of God is, that which is good and acceptable and perfect* (Romans 12:2).

# MEDITATION PROMPTS

- How do you think Paul's concept of *renewing your mind* and biblical meditation are similar?

- Consider the phrase *be transformed by the renewing of your mind*. What does the outcome of this transformation look like in your life?

- Explain how biblical meditation will help you renew your mind.

*Chapter 14*

# SEEING WITH THE EYES OF YOUR HEART

*Contrary to belief, visualization—in the context of biblical meditation—is not unbiblical.* What we teach is that if man chooses what he wants to picture and visualizes that, then that is wrong. If God grants you a dream or a vision, or Jesus paints a parable, or the Bible tells a story, it is not wrong to picture these things. This is essentially what you are doing when you are meditating.

We define "godly imagination" as picturing things the Bible says are true.

## SOME GODLY USES OF THE EYES OF OUR HEARTS

1. God gave Abraham a vision of the stars of the sky and told him he would have that many children (Gen. 15:5), and that produced faith in Abraham's heart (Gen. 15:6). So here we have an example of godly imagery that produced faith in the man who is called the

father of faith (Rom. 4:11). That is a powerful concept. That would indicate that if I wanted faith in my heart which moves mountains, then I would need the same ingredients which God gave to Abraham. These are:

- A spoken promise (Gen. 12:1-2)
- A divine picture (Gen. 15:1,5-6)

Then as I hold this promise and picture it in my heart, meditate on it, and ponder it, God produces a miracle in the fullness of time. For Abraham, a child was born 25 years later.

2.  God has created us with eyes in our hearts with which we can see, picture, and visualize.

3.  God wants to fill these eyes with His dreams, visions, and images (Acts 2:17).

4.  Jesus lived in pictures continuously (John 5:19-20,30).

5.  Jesus filled the eyes of His listeners by constantly teaching with parables (Matt. 13:34).

6.  We are commanded to meditate on the Word, which involves prayerfully rolling it around in our hearts and minds. Because the Bible is full of picture stories, we will by necessity be picturing as we meditate upon Scripture (Josh. 1:8).

7.  When we reason together with God, He uses imagery (Isa. 1:18).

8.  A picture is worth a thousand words, so when I see something, it has the power to change me much more greatly than when I simply think a thought. That is why God says we are transformed (changed) "while we look" (2 Cor. 3:17-18; 4:16–18). When I see myself clothed

with Christ's robe of righteousness (Gal. 3:27), it appears to influence me more greatly than when I simply recall the Scripture verse that says I am the righteousness of God in Christ Jesus (Phil. 3:9).

9.    God counsels us at night through our dreams (Ps. 16:7).

10.   Even the Lord's Supper utilizes imagery. As Jesus broke the bread, He said, "This is My body," and as they drank the wine, He said, "This is My blood" (Matt. 26:26-28). I see this imagery as I partake of the Lord's Supper, and by doing so it impacts me greatly every time I do it.

11.   The Bible is absolutely full of dreams, visions, pictures, images, and parables from cover to cover, so obviously God is big on imagery.

12.   When David prayed, he used imagery (Ps. 23).

13.   When David worshiped, he used imagery (Ps. 36:5-6).

14.   In the Tabernacle in the wilderness, God established much imagery that was an integral part of approaching Him (Exod. 25:8–22).

15    In the New Testament, we are told that Jesus is the Image of the invisible God, and we are to fix our eyes upon Him (Heb. 12:1-2). David was clearly visualizing the Lord at his right hand (Ps. 16:8; Acts 2:25). So in both Old and New Testaments, God has ordained imagery as part of our approach to Him.

## SUMMARY: GODLY USE OF THE EYES OF YOUR HEART

I personally use imagery in all the above ways, and find it extremely beneficial in my Christian walk. God has told me that whatever I fix my eyes on grows within me, and whatever grows within me I become. So instead of fixing my eyes on my sin or my self-effort to become righteous, I fix my eyes on Jesus, and I discover that I become Christlike and find myself radiating His goodness and His glory!

# REFLECT

Describe the process of seeing with the eyes of your heart. How can biblical visualization help you picture the Word of God in a clearer way? Why do you think this is beneficial?

_____

_____

_____

_____

_____

_____

_____

_____

_____

_____

_____

_____

_____

_____

_____

_____

_____

_____

_____

_____

_____

## BIBLICAL VISUALIZATION EXERCISE

Go back through today's segment and select one of the portions of Scripture that was mentioned.

I encourage you to go directly to this passage in the Bible for *yourself.* Either using online Bible study resources or a physical copy of the Scriptures, select the passage and pray to the Holy Spirit for the ability to *see* and *visualize* that portion of the Word like never before. Remember, you are working *with* the Holy Spirit in this process. You are not engaging in an unbiblical practice because your partner, guide, and mentor is the very Spirit of God.

Scripture you selected: _____

Write down what you saw/visualized in the passage you selected.

_____

_____

_____

_____

_____

_____

_____

_____

_____

_____

_____

_____

_____

_____

_____

_____

_____

_____

_____

_____

_____

_____

Write down what specific phrases in the passage of Scripture stood out to you and gave you a picture to visualize.

_____

_____

_____

_____

_____

_____

_____

_____

_____

_____

_____

*Chapter 15*

# MEDITATION, VISUALIZATION, AND IMAGINATION

Your imagination is a canvas that was designed to be painted upon by the brushstrokes of Heaven. When it comes to the importance of imagination and visualization in the meditation process, I often get questions like this:

> **Several in my congregation have asked,** *"Where in the Scriptures are we told to 'picture' or visualize Jesus, as both Second Corinthians 5:6-7 and First Peter 1:7-8 say that we don't see Jesus?"*
>
> *Obviously Hebrews talks about "fixing our eyes on Jesus," but what does that mean? Any advice you can give will be much appreciated.*

## SEEING INWARDLY VERSUS SEEING OUTWARDLY

As you read the context of Second Corinthians 5:6-7 and First Peter 1:7-8, you will note they are both talking about *physically seeing*—seeing *physical circumstances* (2 Cor. 5:6-7) and *physically seeing Jesus* (1 Pet. 1:7-8). When it comes to seeing with the eyes of our hearts, Paul tells us to look and see the glory of the Lord in the "unseen" world (2 Cor. 3:18; 4:18) and Hebrews 12:2 tells us we are to be fixing our eyes on Jesus.

Paul tells us that "we all, with unveiled face, *beholding* as in a mirror the glory of the Lord, *are being transformed* into the same image from glory to glory, just as from the Lord, the Spirit" (2 Cor. 3:18). One chapter later, Paul confirms that this transformation occurs "*while we look* not at the things which are seen, but at the things which are not seen" (2 Cor. 4:18).

*So the question is*: What (or Who) is it in the unseen realm that we are to look at and, that by beholding, will *transform* us into the same image?

> **Your imagination is a canvas that was designed to be painted upon by the brushstrokes of Heaven.**

*The answer*: As I look with the eyes of my heart to see what Jesus is doing in the situation, and I take on His actions by saying, "Yes, Lord," and do what I see Jesus doing, the result is that I am transformed from a person who does something out of self to a person who is doing what I see Jesus doing in the situation.

*For example,* I want to hit someone (maybe just with words, but I want to hit them as they have made me frustrated). But when I look into the spirit world to see how Jesus is reacting to the person, the picture that lights upon my mind is Jesus ministering grace to them. So I decide to minister divine grace to them as well. I decide to do what I see Jesus doing, and thus I have been transformed *while I looked* into the unseen realm, with the eyes of my heart, and observed the actions of Jesus and said "yes" to what He was showing me He was doing.

# SEEING JESUS'S PRESENT-TENSE MOVEMENTS

This is taking us one step beyond the book *In His Steps* by Charles Sheldon where he asked, "What *would* Jesus do?" We ask instead, "What *is* Jesus doing?" Because Jesus is still alive and is Immanuel, God with us, and is still doing things, there is no need to make this a past tense or hypothetical question. It is a present tense question. Jesus is still moving, and we still have eyes in our hearts that function and can see visions and dreams!

# ABIDING IN CHRIST INVOLVES SEEING JESUS

This is the way Christians are to live all the time. It is called *abiding in Christ* (John 15) and it involves hearing, feeling, sensing, and seeing Jesus in action, the One who is walking with us down the road of life. It is simple. It must be simple enough for a child to do (Luke 18:17), so don't make it difficult. It is asking the Holy Spirit to show you what Jesus is doing, and then looking with the eyes of your heart into the unseen world and honoring and accepting and believing the pictures that light upon your mind while you are in that pose. You have asked for them to come from the Holy Spirit, and Jesus's promise is that indeed they do (John 7:37–39; Luke 11:13). So go ahead and accept them in simple child-like faith. Of course they need to be compatible with Scripture, and it is always wisest to submit them for confirmation to your two or three spiritual advisors (Matt. 18:16), especially when involving any significant decisions or if you are uncertain about what you have received.

# WHEN KING DAVID MEDITATED, HE USED THE EYES OF HIS HEART

Notice how King David used the eyes of his heart to "see" the Lord when he was meditating. For example, Psalm 63 associates meditating (Hebrew, *hagah*) with seeing in the Spirit a vision from God (Hebrew, *khazah*).

"I *have seen* (*khazah*) You in the sanctuary, to see Your power and Your glory" (Ps. 63:2). And four verses later: "When I remember You on my bed, I *meditate on* (or "imagine," *hagah be*) You in the night watches" (Ps. 63:6). So for King David, *meditating* absolutely *included seeing* in the Spirit realm. When we meditate, we must also be presenting the eyes of our hearts to the Holy Spirit, asking Him to show us God's visions (Acts 2:17).

In Psalm 16:8 David also indicates he uses vision as he walks down the road of life: "I have *set the Lord continually before me*; because He is at *my right hand,* I will not be shaken."

I would say King David is *picturing the Lord before him, at his right side.* I can think of no reason not to do this. The Bible says Jesus is Immanuel, God with us, so why limit ourselves to just thinking it? Why not picture it? If a picture is worth a thousand words, then what we see has much greater power to impact us than what we hear, probably because we have stepped from mind to heart. I assume that is why *Jesus always painted pictures* when He spoke (Matt. 13:34). He was communicating heart to heart the truths about a heart-to-heart relationship with Almighty God.

# BIBLICAL VISUALIZATION EXERCISE

I want you to reinforce this practice today. Go back through today's segment and select one of the portions of Scripture that was mentioned.

I encourage you to go directly to this passage in the Bible for *yourself.* Either using online Bible study resources or a physical copy of the Scriptures, select the passage and pray to the Holy Spirit for the ability to *see* and *visualize* that portion of the Word like never before. Remember, you are working *with* the Holy Spirit in this process. You are not engaging in an unbiblical practice because your partner, guide, and mentor is the very Spirit of God.

Scripture you selected: _____

Write down what you saw/visualized in the passage you selected.

_____

_____

_____

_____

_____

_____

_____

_____

_____

_____

_____

_____

_____

_____

_____

_____

_____

_____

_____

_____

_____

_____

Write down what specific phrases in the passage of Scripture stood out to you and gave you a picture to visualize.

_____

_____

_____

_____

_____

_____

_____

_____

_____

_____

_____

_____

_____

_____

_____

_____

_____

_____

*Part Five*

# THE SEVEN-STEP
# MEDITATION PROCESS

*But his delight is in the law of the Lord, and in
His law he meditates day and night. He will be like
a tree firmly planted by streams of water, which
yields its fruit in its season and its leaf does not
wither; and in whatever he does, he prospers.*

—PSALM 1:2-3

*"In the inner stillness where meditation leads, the Spirit
secretly anoints the soul and heals our deepest wounds."*

—ST. JOHN OF THE CROSS

# SUCCESS WITH THE SEVEN-STEP MEDITATION PROCESS

*I used this technique and it was one of the most intimate times I have had with the Lord in quite a while. Bottom line: I found this seven-step process very effective and I plan to use it more in the future. Below is a sample journal entry as I used this method.*
—PASTOR JIM FRENCH

Meditation Verse: "*Do not let your heart be troubled; believe in God, believe also in Me*" (John 14:1).

As I meditated on this verse, the Lord showed me a vision of a heart, my heart, which was pierced with arrows. I asked Him what the arrows were and what He wanted to tell me.

## MY JOURNAL ENTRY

This is what I believe the Lord spoke to me:

*Son, our hearts are fused; they are one. But there are some aspects of your heart that you have not completely yielded to Me. I await your decision to do so.*

*The arrows you saw were wounds in your heart from people and events—past hurts and pains. The choice is yours to hold on to them or release them. But if you choose to deal with the wounds yourself, the arrows will remain. Only I can truly remove the arrows and heal the wounds, but you must yield these to Me.*

*Jim, the ministry places you in a position of vulnerability. I ask you to pour your life into people who may not accept you as My servant and messenger. They too have their own pain which will not allow them to trust. In ministering, you must not allow rejection to penetrate your heart.*

*Remember, you were not sent to heal—I was. Your job is to present Me in every situation and any acceptance or rejection is acceptance or rejection of Me. You must make a conscious decision to not accept any rejection or you will be wounded again. The wounds in your heart make it more difficult for Me to minister through you. Yield these wounds and the people who inflicted them to Me and I will heal you.*

Here is my response:

*Yes, Lord. I release these wounds and the people who inflicted them to You. Forgive me for hanging on to them. I repent and ask for Your grace to not allow hurt to penetrate my heart again. Thank You, Lord!*

Chapter 16

# Seven Steps of Biblical Meditation

This is the seven-step process that I personally use when approaching the Scriptures for meditation.

1.  **Write:** I copy the verse by hand onto a piece of paper or 3-by-5 card (Deut. 17:18) and keep it with me to meditate on, memorize, and mutter throughout the day(s). I also record this verse in my meditation journal (which can be written, typed, or verbally recorded).

2.  **Quiet Down**: I become still in God's presence, loving Him through soft soaking music (2 Kings 3:15-16), praying in tongues (1 Cor. 14:14), or putting a smile on my face and picturing Jesus with me (Acts 2:25). I tune to His *flowing* thoughts, pictures, and emotions (John 7:37–39). Our "Sea of Galilee" soaking visualization can assist you in accomplishing this in five minutes: www.cwgministries.org/galilee.

3. **Reason:** I reason together with God (Isa. 1:18), meaning the Spirit guides my reasoning process (through flow). "Lord, what do You want to show me about any of the following: the context of a verse, the Hebrew/Greek definitions of the key words in the verse, any cultural understandings?" (See next chapter, "How to Meditate on a Topic," which details these steps.)

4. **Speak and Imagine**: I ponder the Scripture, speaking it to myself softly over and over again until I can say it with my eyes closed. As I repeat the Scripture, I allow myself to see it with the eyes of my heart. I note what the picture is in my mind's eye as I repeat the Scripture.

5. **Feel** God's Heart: While seeing the above picture, I ask, "Lord, what does this Scripture reveal about Your heart toward me?" I feel His heart and journal it out.

6. **Hear** God's *Rhema*: I put myself in the picture of this Scripture in my mind. I ask, "Lord, what are You speaking to me through this Scripture?" I tune to flowing thoughts and flowing pictures (God's voice and vision) and I record this dialogue in my two-way journaling.

7. **Act**: I accept this revelation, repenting of any sin that is opposite of it and roaring at any obstacle that stands in the way of implementing it. I then speak it forth and act on it.

   ▪ Our hearts burn as Jesus opens Scriptures to us (Luke 24:32).

   ▪ We are transformed as we see what Jesus is doing (2 Cor. 3:18).

The Holy Spirit guides the above process, leading to more or less emphasis on any of the various steps, according to God's desire for the present moment and the personal needs we have. So we remain dependent upon Him throughout.

For example, I may need more or less time to quiet myself in His presence; more or less time in Spirit-led "reasoning"; or more or less time in speaking it, feeling God's heart in it, doing two-way journaling about it, or roaring at the enemy to get his lies out of my head and his hands off my being. So I allow the flow of the Holy Spirit to guide me through the steps of this meditation process.

## YOUR MEDITATION ASSIGNMENT

In the next seven segments, you will interact with each step of the meditation process.

Even though I am providing you with a sample Scripture verse for meditation—to show you how the process works—I encourage you to find your own key verse in Scripture to biblically meditate on for the next seven exercises.

# WRITE

*Record the vision and inscribe it on tablets.*
—HABAKKUK 2:2

Copy the Scripture verse by hand onto a piece of paper or 3-by-5 card (Deut. 17:18) and keep it with you to meditate on, memorize, and mutter throughout the day(s). Also, record the verse in the lined space below.

By the time you are finished with this guided exercise, going through the seven-step process, the goal is for you to have your own meditation journal. There, you can record Scriptures and the revelation you receive while meditating on those passages.

*Choose a Bible verse that you would like to meditate on.*

## REFLECTION FROM DR. VIRKLER

If you do not have a specific Scripture, you can start with Genesis 24:63 and I will help guide you through the meditation process in the upcoming segments.

*Isaac went out to meditate in the field toward evening; and he lifted up his eyes and looked, and behold, camels were coming.*

# JOURNAL

Write down the Scripture verse you choose for the meditation exercise.

_____

_____

_____

_____

_____

_____

_____

_____

_____

_____

_____

_____

_____

_____

_____

_____

_____

# WRITING OUT SCRIPTURE

When you write or type out a verse, you discover words which you otherwise might have missed. Therefore, I write out verses which I know are key truths for my life.

I pray over them, diagram them, analyze them, meditate on them. That is why I have written many of my books. I write so I can learn, so I can put truths I am understanding in my own words and in a framework that is meaningful for me.

The following is the law God gave for new kings who had just been crowned and were coming to sit upon their throne for the first time:

> *Now it shall come about when he sits on the throne of his kingdom, he shall write for himself a copy of this law on a scroll in the presence of the Levitical priests* (Deuteronomy 17:18).

Because we are kings and priests, are we to do any less (1 Peter 2:9)? Let us make writing out the Scriptures an important part of our lives, as this will usher us into new realms of revelation and insight.

# QUIET DOWN

*Surely I have composed and quieted my soul.*
—PSALM 131:2

Become still in God's presence, loving Him through soft soaking/quiet worship music (2 Kings 3:15-16) and/or praying in tongues (1 Cor. 14:14). *Imagine* that Jesus is with you during this process. The Holy Spirit is inside you, desiring to take Truth and turn it into revelation. Tune in to His flowing thoughts, pictures, and emotions (John 7:37–39).

Do *not* journal until after you have become still in His presence. Then you can record the journey through writing. Right now, the key is learning how to quiet yourself down in God's presence and position yourself to meditate on what He is saying to you.

## REFLECTION FROM DR. VIRKLER

With this verse, I used the Sea of Galilee Quieting Exercise, picturing myself together with Jesus and tuned to flow. This exercise is available for free at www.cwgministries.org/galilee.

## JOURNAL

How did the process of *quieting down* go for you today? Describe your journey below.

_____

_____

_____

_____

_____

_____

_____

_____

_____

_____

_____

_____

_____

_____

_____

_____

_____

_____

# Quiet Down

# REASON

*"Come now, and let us reason together," says the Lord.*
—Isaiah 1:18

Now, you will reason together with God about the Scripture. This means that the Holy Spirit will guide your reasoning process (through flow).

Ask questions like, "Lord, what do You want to show me about any of the following?"

- the context of a verse

- the Hebrew/Greek definitions of the key words in the verse

- any cultural understandings

# REFLECTION FROM DR. VIRKLER

Based on the Scripture example, Genesis 24:63, here is a glimpse into my time of reasoning with the Lord. This is what He spoke to my heart during the process:

*Meditation is a lifestyle that I have ordained. Do it in the evening. It is better than watching TV. As you do it, I can and will bring the choicest provisions of life to you. In this case, Isaac lifted up his eyes and saw the gift of his future wife who was being brought to him by his servant. His servant had discovered her in a distant land through a divine appointment. I also bring good gifts to you from distant places while you honor Me by making meditation your lifestyle. For when you honor Me by inviting Me into your everyday life, I honor you by bringing to you divine appointments. Honor Me with your lifestyle. Let your lifestyle be one of ongoing meditation.*

# JOURNAL

Write out what the Lord shares with you as you *reason through* your Scripture verse together with Him.

Be sure to ask the Holy Spirit the questions that are presented above.

_____

_____

_____

_____

_____

_____

_____

# Reason

*Step Four*

# SPEAK AND IMAGINE

Ponder the Scripture, speaking it to yourself softy over and over again until you can say it with your eyes closed.

As you repeat the Scripture, allow yourself to see it with the eyes of your heart. Note what the picture is in your mind's eye as you repeat the Scripture.

## REFLECTION FROM DR. VIRKLER

Based on the Scripture example, Genesis 24:63, this is what I see:

*I see Isaac walking in a field in the evening and pondering as he walks along. I see Jesus at his side, speaking with him.*

## JOURNAL

Write down the pictures that come to your mind as you repeat the Scripture verse to yourself and start to see it with the eyes of your heart.

# FEEL GOD'S HEART

While imagining the Scripture (as outlined in Step Four), ask, "Lord, what does this Scripture reveal about Your heart toward me?" Feel His heart and journal it out.

## REFLECTION FROM DR. VIRKLER

Based on the Scripture example, Genesis 24:63, this is what I feel is God's heart toward me:

> *Mark, I love to walk with you in the cool of the day. This was My original design. This allows you to hear My thoughts and receive My wisdom, My counsel, and My blessing. It is My desire to love you and care for you and provide for you, and this is one key way I can do that if you allow Me to. Come experience My heart toward you in the cool of the day. Come meditate in the cool of the day.*

# JOURNAL

Write down what you feel God's heart *toward you* is through your verse.

_____

_____

_____

_____

_____

_____

_____

_____

_____

_____

_____

_____

_____

_____

_____

_____

_____

_____

_____

_____

# HEAR GOD'S RHEMA

*For the word of God is living and active and
sharper than any two-edged sword.*
—HEBREWS 4:12

Put yourself in the picture of this Scripture in your mind.

Ask, "Lord, what are You speaking to me through this Scripture?"
Tune to the flowing thoughts and flowing pictures (God's voice and
vision) and record this dialogue in your two-way journaling.

## REFLECTION FROM DR. VIRKLER

Based on the Scripture example, Genesis 24:63, this is what I
believe God is actively speaking to me:

> *Mark, there is **so** much I want to reveal to you, and I do it
> as we take these walks together in the cool of the day. You see,
> this was My pattern in the Garden of Eden. I chose for it to
> be our pattern also, that we walk together down the road of*

*life. Will you come to Me in the cool of the day and meditate in My presence, allowing Me to minister grace to you on a daily basis? You can ponder the specific needs and situations you are surrounded by and present them to Me, and I will give you revelation and insight as to how to best handle them and respond to them. I will do this daily if you will walk with Me daily. You will experience ideas and understanding beyond your natural ability. You will accomplish beyond your natural giftings.*

# JOURNAL

Write down and record what the Lord is actively speaking to you about your Scripture verse.

_____

_____

_____

_____

_____

_____

_____

_____

_____

_____

_____

_____

_____

_____

*Step Seven*

# ACT

*Blessed are those who hear the word of God and observe it.*
—LUKE 11:28

Accept the revelation God is speaking to you and repent of any sin that is opposite of it. Repentance is twofold. While it involves experiencing godly sorrow over our sin, it also transforms the way we think. The Holy Spirit is inviting you to adjust the way you think—and ultimately the way you live—to come into alignment with His revelation.

Speak it forth and then act on it! Meditation is all about producing a lifestyle where we start living out the Word of God.

## REFLECTION FROM DR. VIRKLER

Here is an example of what I have prayed back to the Lord in response to His revelation:

*Lord, I accept this awesome invitation from You, my Lord and my Redeemer. What a gracious gift You have offered me, and all I have to do is say yes and we walk together. I receive Your life and fullness into my heart and life. Lord, what an amazing offer You are making. I roar at every false belief that I can do it on my own. That is a lie from satan. I renounce humanism and rationalism. Get out of my life, now! I choose to die daily and come alive only to Jesus, who is my life.*

*Lord, I will walk with You and talk with You in the cool of the day, and I will present to You the issues I am facing and ask for Your wisdom and insight on them. I thank You, Lord, for Your gracious wisdom, revelation, and strength which flow so freely!*

# JOURNAL

Write down your response to God's revelation in the form of an *action prayer*.

Ask the Lord how He wants you to integrate this meditation into your everyday life and then purpose in your spirit to do it.

*Part Six*

# MISTAKES TO AVOID IN BIBLICAL MEDITATION

# Twelve Mistakes to Avoid When Meditating

This section is here simply to provide safeguards against false or ineffective approaches to biblical meditation. Below, I will list twelve common mistakes people make when it comes to meditating.

**Mistake 1:** Settling for the western approach to "study," which is generally defined by man controlling one faculty within his mind (i.e. reason), while biblical meditation is a much more complete process and is defined as the Holy Spirit controlling all faculties within one's heart and mind.

**Mistake 2:** Being afraid of the word *meditation* even though it is a word used many times in Scripture.

**Mistake 3:** Looking to the false gods of self or a New Age god rather than fixing my eyes on Jesus and asking the Holy Spirit to guide the meditations of my heart.

**Mistake 4:** Thinking the meditation process taught in Scripture is only to be applied to Scripture, and not understand that we are to meditate on all areas of life: on God's works, His creation, and in **everything** we do or explore. With His Spirit at our side as we meditate, our search will reveal divine revelation, and not just man's thoughts. Einstein said, "I want to know God's thoughts, the rest are details."

**Mistake 5:** Meditating on satan and his works or the wickedness of mankind and his works. Instead, only meditate on God and His works, which results in keeping us full of faith, hope, and love.

**Mistake 6:** Not knowing how to clearly define God's voice and vision, which are recognized as flowing thoughts and flowing pictures. Not knowing that I can enlarge this revelation by recording in my journal the flow as it is coming (as taught in detail in the book *4 Keys to Hearing God's Voice*).

**Mistake 7:** Thinking the goal of meditation is achieving stillness rather than realizing that we step through our stillness to the Lord's revelation and power. The goal is connecting with Almighty God.

**Mistake 8:** Expressing pride as I try to prove my position is right rather than expressing meekness, which is having a willingness to change my mind no matter what the cost.

**Mistake 9:** Not being willing to explore in depth all Scriptures on every side of a topic, but looking only for verses which support my preconceived position.

**Mistake 10:** Taking the accuser's attitude, which is satan's, rather than the Comforter's attitude, which is the Holy Spirit's, and thus coming against people (or self) rather than alongside them.

**Mistake 11:** Making meditation something harder than what a child can do.

**Mistake 12:** Making meditation an ironclad, mechanical, seven-step process rather than a flexible approach guided by the Holy Spirit.

# DOES STUDYING THE BIBLE EARN GOD'S APPROVAL?

The command, "Study to show yourself approved" is actually a mistranslation of the Greek text. Most translations other than the King James translate the Greek word *spoudazo* as something other than "study." *Spoudazo* appears twelve times in the New Testament, and only this once is translated as "study." The New King James version translates Second Timothy 2:15 correctly:

> *Be diligent to present yourself approved to God, a worker who does not need to be ashamed, rightly dividing the word of truth* (2 Timothy 2:15 NKJV).

The Bible contains no other command to study the Bible, which is quite shocking. Although Luke was doing careful investigation in the preparation of the writing of his Gospel (Luke 1:1-3), the Bible makes it crystal clear that the Spirit was also guiding him (2 Tim. 3:16).

About half the Bible translations say Ezra "studied" the Law (Ezra 7:10), but the other half say Ezra set his heart to *seek* the Law of the Lord. The Hebrew word used here is *dârash*.[1] It shows up 160 times and is only translated "study" this one time. It is most generally translated "to seek or to inquire," so I surely feel Ezra had an inquiring heart that was seeking after God, and thus he was doing more than simple mental rational study of the Law of God. He was seeking God for revelation and insight.

What the Bible does command, many times, is that *you meditate on the Bible.*

## NOTE

1.  James Strong, *Strong's Exhaustive Concordance* (Peabody, MA: Hendrickson Publishers, 2007), H1875.

# Chapter 19

# AVOID THE MINISTRY OF CONDEMNATION AND DEATH

The Bible can be studied improperly. It can be used to minister condemnation and death (2 Cor. 3:6–9), and the Pharisees, who studied the Bible intensely, used their wrong interpretation of Bible passages to have Jesus killed.

Paul completed his Bible school career (Acts 8:1-3), and then he too used his wrong Bible knowledge to go out and kill Christians. I did much the same after I completed Bible college. I verbally attacked and "killed" Christians with whom I disagreed. In each of these cases we were using the Bible without the Spirit and producing death and not life (2 Cor. 3:7–9).

Paul had a spiritual encounter with God (Acts 9:1–18) and then spent three years in the Arabian wilderness receiving "revelation knowledge" (Gal. 1:17), which He called "true knowledge" (Col. 2:2; 3:10) and put in contrast with "knowledge." His evaluation was that his previous Bible study was dung (Phil. 3:1–10). Wow!

# RESIST THE
# REASONING OF MAN

Webster states that *study* is the "application of the mental faculties to the acquisition of knowledge." In other words, *I* decide what *I* want to research, which tools *I* will use as *I* research, what *I* am hoping to discover, and when *I* have found it. *I* am in the center of the process, guiding its every step. *I* use the principles of inductive Bible study. *I* decide when *I* have truth.

This would be a violation of Scripture and thus a sin to be repented of, as the Bible clearly says the flesh profits nothing (John 6:63) and the entire process just described was the effort of my flesh. Instead, we are to be like Jesus who did nothing of His own initiative (John 8:28).

It was satan who tempted Eve with this particular sin, saying *you* can *know* (Gen. 3:5). "You" became humanism, and "know" became rationalism. In embracing this lie, man descended from regular walks with God in the cool of the day, where God granted him daily revelation, to the darkness of man's limited thoughts.

The Bible is crystal clear that man's thoughts are not God's thoughts (Isa. 55:8-9). So I surely never want to begin, continue, or end any process with the efforts of my flesh or with the exertion of my thoughts in the center of the process, for if I do I will enter into death and not life.

# AFTERWORD

This work is not intended to be the definitive teaching on biblical meditation. There are some excellent resources available for you to study the topic further. However, you will find that biblical meditation is best learned…and practiced!

My goal in this *Hearing God* series is to give you practical handbooks that teach and also train. I want to offer you information *with* interaction so you can start to experience transformation.

If you would like to study the concept of biblical meditation deeper—from this interactive approach—I would encourage you to participate in the study *Discover the Lost Art of Biblical Meditation* available in Christian Leadership University's *School of the Spirit*: www.cluschoolofthespirit.com/meditation.

You will find more information about this course in the back of the book.

# WESTERN STUDY VERSUS BIBLICAL MEDITATION

## STUDY (GREEK/WESTERN)

*"Application of the mental faculties to the acquisition of knowledge"* (Webster).

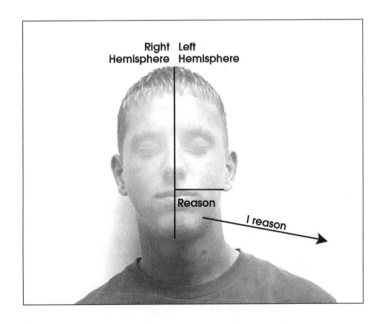

### Study (my use of one part of one hemisphere of my brain):

1. Is nowhere endorsed in Scripture (2 Tim. 2:15 is a mistranslation in the King James Bible).

2. Is self in action (i.e. humanism—a false god).

3. Is self using reason (i.e. rationalism—a false god).

4. Results in wisdom from below—earthly, natural, or demonic (James 3:15). For example, reason caused Peter to be at odds with the purposes of God (John 18:10-11).

### Study violates the following biblical principles:

1. Galatians 2:20—I resurrect self, which no longer lives.

2. Romans 12:1—I am using my faculties rather than presenting them to God to use.

3. Isaiah 1:18—I am reasoning, rather than reasoning together with God.

4. Genesis 3:5—I've fallen prey to the temptation of the Garden of Eden that I can know good and evil.

# MEDITATION (HEBREW/LAMAD)

*"To murmur; to converse with oneself, and hence aloud; speak; talk; babbling; communication; mutter; roar; mourn; a murmuring sound; i.e., a musical notation; to study; to ponder; revolve in the mind; imagine; pray; prayer; reflection; devotion"* (Strong's Exhaustive Concordance).

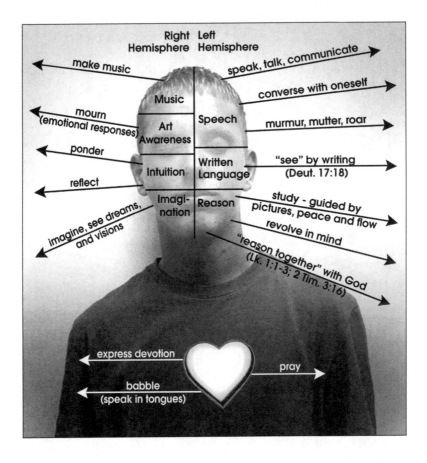

*Meditation (God's use of every part of both hemispheres of my brain as He fills and flows out through my heart by His Spirit):*

1.  Is endorsed 18 times in the King James Bible.

2.  Is God in action within the individual.

3.  Is God granting revelation through the heart and mind that have been yielded to Him.

4.  Results in wisdom from above—pure, peaceable, gentle (James 3:17).

### *Meditation applies the following biblical principles:*

1.  Galatians 2:20—I let Christ live through me.

2.  Romans 12:1—I am yielding my outer faculties to the indwelling Spirit (i.e., to "flow," John 7:38).

3.  Isaiah 11:2—When reasoning together with God, I receive a spirit of wisdom and understanding and knowledge.

4.  John 5:19-20,30—I'm living as Jesus did, out of divine initiative, doing what I see and hear my Father doing.

# THE HEBREW AND GREEK
# WORDS FOR MEDITATION

Let us explore the precise definition of each of the Hebrew and Greek words for meditation.

### *hâgâh (H1897) haw-gaw'*

- *Strong's Exhaustive Concordance* definition: to murmur (in pleasure or anger); to ponder, imagine, meditate, mourn, mutter, roar, speak, study, talk, utter

- *Brown-Driver-Briggs* definition: to moan, growl, utter, muse, mutter, meditate, devise, plot, speak, roar, groan, imagine

- *King James Concordance*—Total KJV occurrences of H1897: 24, which are translated as:
  - ✓ meditate—6 (Joshua 1:8, Psalm 1:2, Psalm 63:6, Psalm 77:12, Psalm 143:5, Isaiah 33:18)

- ✓ mourn—4 (Isaiah 16:7, Isaiah 38:14, Isaiah 59:11, Jeremiah 48:31)
- ✓ speak—3 (Psalm 35:28, Proverbs 8:7)
- ✓ imagine—2 (Psalm 2:1, Psalm 38:12)
- ✓ studieth—2 (Proverbs 15:28, Proverbs 24:2)
- ✓ mutter—1 (Isaiah 8:19)
- ✓ muttered—1 (Isaiah 59:3)
- ✓ roaring—1 (Isaiah 31:3-4 (2))
- ✓ speaketh—1 (Psalm 37:30)
- ✓ talk—1 (Psalm 71:24)
- ✓ utter—1 (Job 27:4)
- ✓ uttering—1 (Isaiah 59:13)

### śîychâh (H7881) see-khaw'

- *Strong's Exhaustive Concordance* definition: reflection, devotion, meditation, prayer

- *Brown-Driver-Briggs* definition: meditation, reflection, prayer, devotion, complaint, musing, study

- *King James Concordance*—Total KJV occurrences: 2, which are translated as:
  - ✓ meditation—2 (Psalm 119:97, Psalm 119:99)

### higgâyôn (H1902) hig-gaw-yone'

- *Strong's Exhaustive Concordance* definition: a murmuring sound, a musical notation, meditation, solemn sound

- *Brown-Driver-Briggs* definition: meditation, resounding music, musing, plotting

- *King James Concordance*—Total KJV occurrences: 4, which are translated as:
  - ✓ device—1 (Lamentations 3:62)
  - ✓ *higgaion*—1 (not translated, Psalm 9:16)
  - ✓ meditation—1 (Psalm 19:14)
  - ✓ sound—1 (Psalm 92:3)

### śiyach (H7878) see'-akh (A primitive root)

- *Strong's Exhaustive Concordance* definition: to ponder, converse (with oneself, and hence aloud), utter, commune, complain, declare, meditate, muse, pray, speak, talk

- *Brown-Driver-Briggs* definition: to put forth, meditate, muse, commune, speak, complain, ponder, sing, to complain, to talk, consider, put forth thoughts

- *King James Concordance*—Total KJV occurrences: 21, which are translated as:
  - ✓ meditate—5 (Psalm 119:15, Psalm 119:23, Psalm 119:48, Psalm 119:78, Psalm 119:148)
  - ✓ talk—5 (1 Chronicles 16:9, Psalm 77:12, Psalm 105:2, Psalm 119:27, Proverbs 6:22)
  - ✓ speak—4 (Judges 5:10, Job 12:8, Psalm 69:12, Psalm 145:5)
  - ✓ commune—1 (Psalm 77:5-6)
  - ✓ complain—1 (Job 7:11)
  - ✓ complained—1 (Psalm 77:3)
  - ✓ declare—1 (Isaiah 53:8)
  - ✓ muse—1 (Psalm 143:5)
  - ✓ pray—1 (Psalm 55:17)
  - ✓ prayer—1 (Job 15:4)

### *siyach (H7879) see'-akh (From the root word H7878, same spelling)*

- *Strong's Exhaustive Concordance* definition: contemplation, utterance, babbling, communication, complaint, meditation, prayer, talk

- *Brown-Driver-Briggs* definition: meditation, complaint, musing, plaint, complaint, musing, anxiety, trouble, talk

- *King James Concordance*—Total KJV occurrences: 14, which are translated as:
  - ✓ complaint—9 (1 Samuel 1:16, Job 7:13, Job 9:27, Job 10:1, Job 21:4, Psalm 55:2, Psalm 142:1-2)
  - ✓ babbling—1 (Proverbs 23:29)
  - ✓ communication—1 (2 Kings 9:11)
  - ✓ meditation—1 (Psalm 104:34)
  - ✓ prayer—1 (Psalm 64:1)
  - ✓ talking—1 (1 Kings 18:27)

### *meletaō (G3191) mel-et-ah'-o*

- *Strong's Exhaustive Concordance* definition: to take care of, revolve in the mind, imagine

- *Thayer's Greek Definitions*: to care for, attend to carefully, practice, to meditate, devise, contrive

- *King James Concordance*—Total KJV occurrences: 3, which are translated as:
  - ✓ imagine—1 (Acts 4:25)
  - ✓ meditate—1 (1 Timothy 4:15)
  - ✓ premeditate—1 (Mark 13:11)

Appendix C

# MAN'S DOCTRINE VERSUS SOUND DOCTRINE

## SOUND DOCTRINE INCORPORATES:

1. The humble in heart seeking God (Matt. 5:8)

2. Receiving enlightenment from God (1 John 2:8)

3. Growing in faith and love (Gal. 5:6)

4. Being transformed by the power of the Holy Spirit (1 John 2:9)

5. Within the context of life and community (2 Cor. 13:1; Acts 15)

# MAN'S DOCTRINE VERSUS SOUND DOCTRINE

| Characteristics of Man's Doctrine: begins, continues, and ends with reason | Characteristics of Sound Doctrine: begins, continues, and ends with the Spirit |
| --- | --- |
| Man's conceptualization of biblical truth (Mark 7:6-7) | Revelation—knowledge truth (Phil. 3:1–10, 1 Cor. 2:9-10, John 5:19-20,30) |
| Changes with current trends (Eph. 4:14–15) | Promotes a growth in intimacy with Christ (Eph. 4:14–15) |
| Myths, genealogies, speculation (1 Tim. 1:3–5) | Promotes love from a pure heart, good conscience, and sincere faith (1 Tim. 1:3–5) |
| Encompasses worldly fables (1 Tim. 4:7) | Disciplines for the purpose of godliness (1 Tim. 4:7, 1 Tim. 6:1–6) |
| Produces envy, strife, abusive language, evil suspicions, and constant friction (1 Tim. 6:1–6) | Produces godliness and contentment (1 Tim. 6:6) |

# DOCTRINES COME FROM EITHER SATAN OR GOD

| Where man's doctrine comes from | Where divine doctrine comes from |
| --- | --- |
| From demons, from deceitful spirits (1 Tim. 4:1–7) | From above (James 3:17) |

# THE CONDITION OF ONE'S HEART IS CRUCIAL IN COMING TO TRUTH

| | Characteristics of those who promote man's doctrine—impure hearts | Characteristics of those who promote divine doctrine—pure hearts |
|---|---|---|
| 1 | Hypocritical liars, seared consciences (1 Tim. 4:1–7) | Show reverence, honor, and respect (1 Tim. 6:1–6) |
| 2 | Conceited, understand nothing; morbid interest in controversial questions and disputes about words (1 Tim. 6:1–6) | Hold fast the faithful word which is in accordance with sound teaching, and able to exhort in sound doctrine and refute those who contradict (Titus 1:9–16) |
| 3 | Men of depraved mind and deprived of the truth (1 Tim. 6:1–6) | Men with pure minds (Titus 1:15) |
| 4 | Teach for money (1 Tim. 6:1–6, Titus 1:9–16) | Teach because they love the truth (2 Thess. 2:10) |
| 5 | Teach to tickle people's ears (2 Tim. 4:3–4) | Teach what the Holy Spirit gives (John 7:16–17) |
| 6 | Rebellious men, empty talkers and deceivers, teaching spirituality through works (Titus 1:9–16) | Spirituality is through grace alone (Eph. 2:9) |
| 7 | Defiled and unbelieving—thus nothing is pure to them (Titus 1:9–16) | Believing and pure—thus all is pure to them (Titus 1:9–16) |
| 8 | Seek their own glory (John 7:18) | Seek the glory of God (John 7:18) |

## NOTE

1.  For more information, see: www.cwgministries.org/doctrine.

# Art of Biblical Meditation Course

## EXPERIENCE SCRIPTURE
### ALIVE, PULSATING, QUICKENED—**EVERY DAY**

*Were not our hearts burning within us while he talked with us on the road and opened the Scriptures to us?* (Luke 24:32 NIV)

Through The *Art of Biblical Meditation Course* you will experience your heart burning with revelation, just as the disciples did on the Emmaus road. We will train you in the following three skills:

- ☑ *The art of biblical meditation,* which is far deeper and more engaging than western study. Meditation involves your heart utilizing both hemispheres of your mind.

- ☑ *A review of how to hear God's voice,* which allows the Holy Spirit to be at your side, guiding and illuminating your heart and mind as you examine Scripture.

- ☑ *Use of an electronic Bible research software package,* which allows you to explore the Bible in depth, conducting comprehensive, contemporary research from the original Hebrew and Greek.

You are going to have fun and get truly excited as you discover how easy and addictive biblical meditation can be!

VISIT:
www.cluschooloftthespirit.com/meditation

# Interactive Online Training from CLU School of the Spirit

**Exploring the #1 free Bible software program in the world**

- ☑ We will train you how to set up and use e-Sword, a free Bible software program that has been downloaded over 25 million times in 240 countries. e-Sword makes it effortless to discover the exact meanings of words in their original languages, and to find every verse in the Bible which has that specific Greek or Hebrew word in it. Wow! All this at the touch of a button!

**We coach you in conducting Bible meditations on TWO topics**

- ☑ We will guide you in completing a meditation on the topic of "Biblical Meditation," using e-Sword, to make the research a snap.
- ☑ Then we will let you review *our* meditation on biblical Meditation so you can **compare your insights with ours.**
- ☑ Finally, we will coach you in doing a Bible meditation on a topic/area God is asking *you* to master.

***Look at ALL you will receive*** in this interactive Spirit Life Training Module!

- ☑ Complete set of training videos
- ☑ Downloadable MP3 audio
- ☑ Complete PDF e-book
- ☑ Step-by-step guidance from the Interactive Learning Management System
- ☑ Certificate of Completion awarding 5 CEUs
- ☑ Coaching

**www.cluschoolofthespirit.com/meditation**

# Discover More from Mark Virkler

*Your How-To Coach for the Spirit-Led Life*

Mark and Patti Virkler have **written 60 books** demonstrating how to take God's voice into area after area of life. These are available at: www.cwgministries.org/catalog.

They have also developed **over 100 college courses** for Christian Leadership University that put the voice of God in the center of your learning experience. These classes can all be taken from your home. View the complete catalog online at: www.cluonline.com.

Get started with a lighter, completely **online version of the course** from School of the Spirit: www.cluschoolofthespirit.com /meditation.

Would you allow the Virklers to recommend **a coach to guide you** in applying God's voice in every area of your life? Information about their Personal Spiritual Trainer program is available at: www .cwgministries.org/pst.

We invite you to **become a certified facilitator** of this course and teach others to hear God's voice! Find out the details at: www .cwgministries.org/certified.

You can even host Mark Virkler in your community for **a weekend seminar** on "How to Hear God's Voice." Details can be found at: www.cwgministries.org/seminars.

Get — **FREE** E-BOOKS *every week!*

LOVE to READ club

# JOIN *the* CLUB

As a member of the **Love to Read Club,** receive exclusive offers for FREE, 99¢ and $1.99 e-books* every week. Plus, get the **latest news** about upcoming releases from **top authors** like these...

**DESTINYIMAGE.COM/FREEBOOKS**

| T.D. JAKES | BILL JOHNSON | CINDY TRIMM | JIM STOVALL | BENI JOHNSON | MYLES MUNROE |

**LOVE to READ** club

DESTINY IMAGE